VALAIS
Switzerland

AN UNDISCOVERED SWISS CANTON

Farrol Kahn

Farrol Kahn

Farrol Kahn is the author of several
books including Riga and its beaches
(Landmark Visitors Guide), Oxford
(Landmark Visitors Guide) and Arrive
in Better Shape (HarperPaperbacks).
He lives in the Valais, Switzerland.

Published by Valais Guides
Farrol Kahn GmbH,
Eischoll, CH-3943
Switzerland

Email; fkahn@aviation-health.co.uk
Website: www.valaisguide.co.uk
Tel: +41 (0) 27 934 1721
Mob: +41 (0) 794218981

ISBN 978-3-033-02934-7
© Farrol Kahn 2011

Editor: Natasha Kahn
Editorial Assistant: Ilse Carlen
Print: Gutenberg Press Ltd, Malta
Design, Maps: AZZZA Limited,
www.azzza.eu

Acknowledgments

The author would like to thank his Editorial assistant, Ilse Carlen for her prodigious effort and the team of his daughter Natasha, Anita Zabilevska and Paul Bizzell. Also those who have kindly provided illustrations and photographs. A big thanks to Bruno Huggler and Valais Tourisme; John and Sheila Cosford; Sierre-Anniviers Tourisme; Sion Tourisme, St-Maurice Tourisme; Bouveret Tourisme; Grimentz/St-Jean Tourisme; Lötschental Tourismus; Nendaz tourisme; Tourisme de Savièse; Vercorin Tourisme; Pfyn-Finges Naturpark; Stockalperturm; Vinea; Les Vins du Valais; TMR Mont Blanc Express; Musée St Bernard; Gästecenter Obergoms; Fondation Pierre Gianadda; Monika Pfaffen; Renato Jordan; Angelica Brunner; Brigitte Wolf; Christophe Venetz; Marie-Claude Morand; Susanne Briand; Sylvie Zumofen; Suzanne Huesser; Natural History Museum, Geneva; among others including Singleton.

Photo Credits: Front Cover Photo: Kurt Müller; Back Cover Photos: Simplon Tourismus; Lötschental Tourismus; © www.alessandrameniconzi.com; Valais Tourisme 4; Farrol Kahn 4; Val d'Hérens Tourisme 4; Musée et Chiens du Saint-Bernard 4; Les Vins du Valais, Giorgio Skory (2008) 8; Val d'Hérens Tourisme, Pascal Charlet 10; Heidadorf, Visperterminen Tourist Office 11; Reckingen-Gluringen Tourismus 12; Nendaz Tourisme 13; Pierre Gianadda Fondation 14; Renato Jordan 16; Farrol Kahn 18; Grimentz/St-Jean Tourisme 19; Les Vins du Valais, Giorgio Skory 2008 20; Ferme Pédagogique "Au Coeur du Valais" 20; Médiatheque Martigny 22; © MVVV – E. Roux 22; Sion Tourisme 23; Les Fils de Charles Favre SA 23; Farrol Kahn 24; Adrian Mathier 26; John Cosford 28; Valais Tourisme 29; Carlen Philipp Belvedere hotel 32; John Cosford 35; Gästecenter Obergoms 35; Reckingen-Gluringen Tourismus 36; Gästecenter Obergoms 36; John Cosford 38; Brigitte Wolf 38; Musées Cantonaux, Sion Robert Barradi 39; Angelica Brunner Valrando 40; Angelica Brunner Valrando 41; Eggishorn Tourismus 41; Eggishorn Tourismus 42; Angelica Brunner Valrando 43; John Cosford 44; Simplon Tourismus 46; Peter Salzmann 46; Museum Stockalperschloss, Arthur Huber 47; Stockalper Tower hotel restaurant 48; Simplon Tourismus 49; Simplon Tourismus 50; Lötschental Tourismus 52; Lötschnetal Tourismus 54; Walter Jaggy 54; Farrol Kahn 55; Monika Pfaffen 56; Monika Pfaffen 57; Leukerbad Tourismus 58; Leukerbad Tourismus 59; Leukerbad Tourismus 60; Leukerbad Tourismus 61; Sani Fattorini Albinen Tourismus 62; Sani Fattorini Albinen Tourismus 63; Musées Cantonaux, Sion, Robert Barradi 64; Leuk Tourismus 65; Leuk Tourismus 66; Leuk Tourismus 68; Pfyn-Finges Nature Reserve 69; Anita Zabilevska 70; Association VINEA 72; Christophe Venetz 72; Farrol Kahn 72; Roland Gerth 73; Valais Tourisme 74; Vercorin Tourisme 74; Valais Tourisme 75; Grimentz/St Jean Tourisme 75; Anita Zabilevska 76; Brigitte Wolf 77; Val d'Hérens Tourisme 78; Musées Cantonaux, Sion Robert Barradi 80; Sion Tourisme 81; Sion Tourisme 82; Musées Cantonaux, Sion Robert Barradi 83; Sion Tourisme 83; Grande Dixence SA 84; Farrol Kahn 84; Valais Tourisme 85; Christophe Valentini, Canton Valais 86; Martigny Tourisme 88; TMR SA 89; Grande Dixence SA 90; L. Cavin, Natural History Museum of the City of Geneva 90; Valais Tourisme 92; Bouveret Tourisme 94; Monika Pfaffen 96; Grégoire Montagero 97; Grégoire Montagero 98; Chablais Tourisme 100; Courtauld Gallery, London. Gordon H. Roberton, A. C. Cooper 102; Chamonix Tourisme Mario Colonel 104; Chamonix Tourisme Mario Colonel 105; Vinea 153; Suzanne Huesser 160.

Contents

Chapter 1:

The Valais in context

Chapter 2:

The Regions

Chapter 3:

Fact File

The Valais

Lake Geneva
St. Gingolph
Le Bouveret
Monthey
Salgesch
Montana
Sierre
Chalais
Vercorin
Sion
Conthey
St. Maurice
Val d'Illiez
Champéry
Val d'Anniviers
Vallon d'Réchy
Maya Noble
8707ft
St Luc
Vissoie
Dents du Midi
10685ft
Rhône
Nendaz
Grimentz
Vernayaz
Fully
Salvan
Becs de Bosson
10331ft
Finhaut
Martigny
Verbier
Evolène
Trient
FRANCE
Osière
Dent Blanche
14294ft
Argentière
Praz de-Fort
Arolla
Val Ferret
Bourg St. Pierre
Charmonix
Ferret
Ferret
9770ft
ITALY
Mont Blanc
15770ft
Grand St. Bernard
Pass

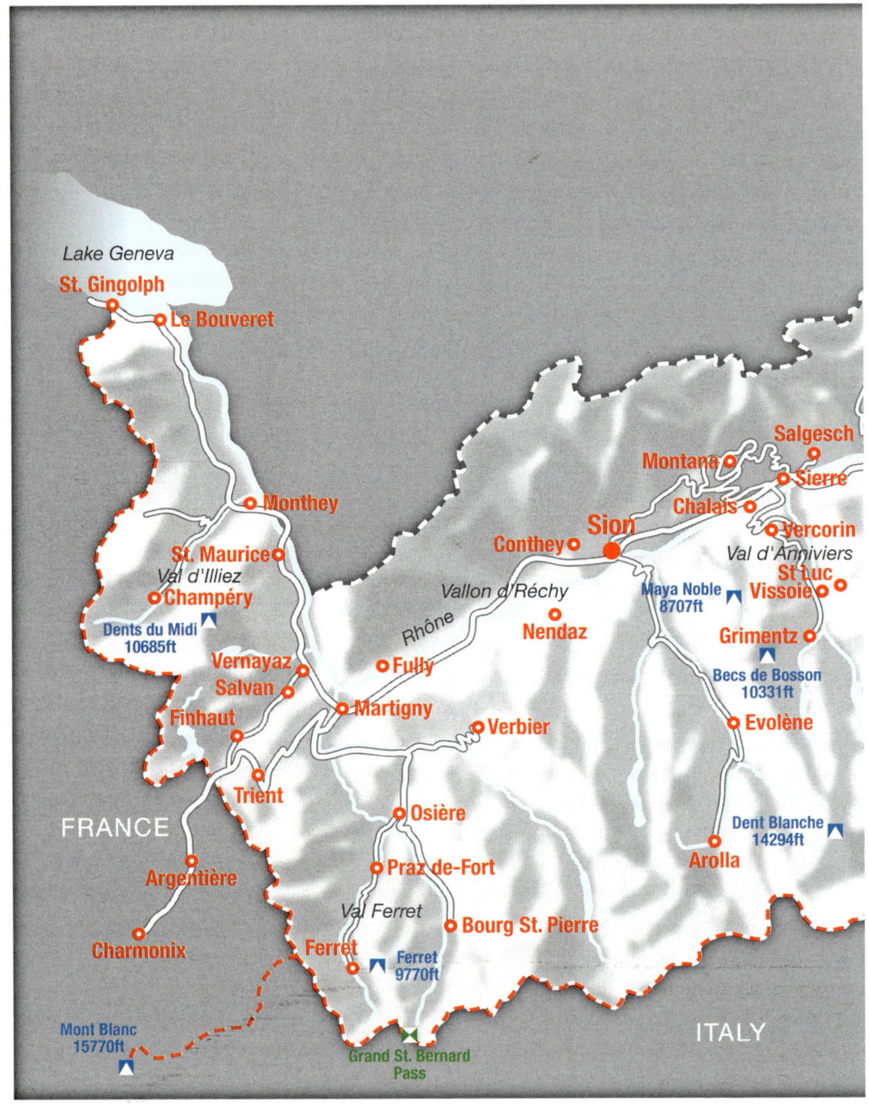

The Valais

Rhone Glacier
Gletsch
Grimsel Pass
Oberwald
Münster
Reckingen
Nufenen Pass
Aletschorn 13763ft
Lötschental (Lötschen) valley
Eggishorn 9603ft
The Goms
Blinnenhorn 11069ft
Fafleralp
Blatten
Ried
Breithorn 12417ft
Torrenthorn 9835ft
Wiler
Kippel
Nesthorn 12545ft
Ernen
Flesch
Leukerbad
Bieschhorn 12906ft
Bettmeralp
Ofenhorn 10613ft
Goppenstein
Riederalp
Binn
Albinen
Leuk
Naters
Brig
Bättlihorn 9681ft
Turtmann
Visp
Simplon Pass
ITALY
Bella Tola 9927ft
Grächen
Breithorn 11089ft
Gondo
Bishorn 13123ft
Weisshorn 14780ft
Saas Fee
Domodossola
Zinalrothorn 13848ft
Zermatt
N
Matterhorn 14691ft
Breithorn 13661ft
0   10 km
1000 ft = 304.8 m

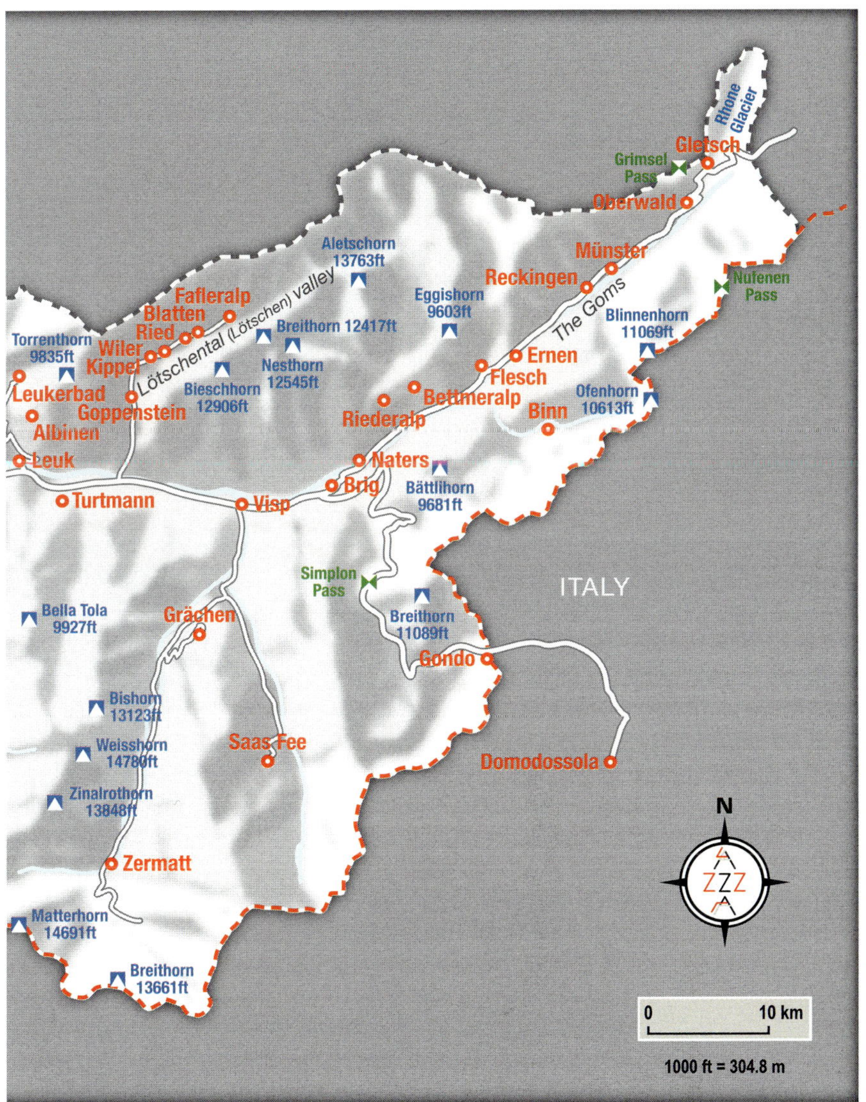

Chapter 1

The Valais in context

When most people first come to the Valais they are only aware of the famous resorts of Zermatt, Verbier, Crans-Montana and Saas-Fee, and oblivious to its other undiscovered side which is just as interesting. There are historic towns, thermal baths, a Roman amphitheatre, dinosaur footprints, gold mines, minerals, an ancient monastery, many deep rural side valleys of great scenic beauty and just plain wacky things. It's rich in culture and tradition and is great for skiing, climbing and hiking.

History

The Valais is Switzerland's third largest canton and it entered the Swiss confederation in 1815. It's the most isolated Alpine district and is predominantly Catholic. Two-thirds of the population are French-speaking, the rest German-speaking. The French area runs from Bouveret on Lake Geneva in the west to Sierre, and the Swiss-German area from Salgesch to Gletch in the east. The Romans conquered the Celts of the lower Valais, leaving behind them the legacy of Latin civilisation. The Upper Valais was invaded during the 6th century by Germanic peoples, the Walsers, tribes who remained unconquered and spoke a Swiss-German dialect.

One of the first things you discover is the invisible border between the two areas. Neither the French nor the German speakers – who call the canton Wallis – are interested in the culture of the other. The capital, Sion, is in the French part and appears very French.

The river Rhone runs through the Valais fed by glaciers (which cover 20% of the canton). Its dry climate – the surrounding mountains prevent access to rain bearing winds – means it has the most sunshine in the whole of Switzerland. The hot summers and cold winters, with springs tempered by the warm dry föhn blowing up from the Mediterranean, mean the climate is favourable to viniculture. Wines flourish on the rugged, sun-baked ridges of the south-facing slopes.

The paucity of rain and the torrents of water in the inaccessible gorges led to the development of an irrigation system that showed the tenacity and inventive spirit of the Valaisians. The network of narrow channels, 'bisses' in French and 'suonen' in Swiss-German, weave a cat's cradle over the foothills of the high mountains.

Two traditions predominate in Valaisian communities. The first is the annual trek

Cow fighting in Val d'Hérens.

of cows, sheep or goats to the summer pastures high in the Alps, and then in the winter down to the sheltered barns of the villages. Cow fights developed from this custom. It's not as gory as Spanish bullfighting as the aim is to see which cow is best suited to lead the herds in the summer pastures. Without these fights cows would fight among themselves, leading to serious injuries or even death. Herens or Eringer (German) breeds of cattle are sturdy and muscular with curved horns and a lively, belligerent character. They are good for both milk and meat.

The springtime contests which decide the leader are tame affairs. Heads are lowered and horns locked before the struggle begins. The weaker cow finally retreats, chased by the winner. Organised fights are arranged to determine regional and cantonal winners. The final contest is called Combats des Reines and is held in the Roman amphitheatre in Martigny. The winner means big money for the farmer as he can be assured of a head price of 60,000 – 80,000 francs.

The second important tradition is the sacred festival. The Corpus Christi pageant is the highlight of the festive calendar. It's devoted to the Eucharist which is held on the second Thursday after Pentecost. The occasion is celebrated by the whole village. There's a ritualistic procession led by the men dressed as 'red' soldiers. Wearing old uniforms and carrying ancient rifles, they are followed by women in their traditional village or cantonal costumes and finally, the village band and choir.

Guggenmusik, Chimbilagos from Visperterminen.

The carnival is also celebrated in the Valais and each village has its own version. In Lötschental there is the Tschäggättä (masked people), in Evolène the Peluches (soft cuddly toys) and the modern urban equivalent, Guggenmusik, in which members of a band dress up.

It's worth exploring villages on both sides of the Valais – the effort will be rewarded by the natural beauty, the roaring torrents of pure glacier water, the unforgettable alpine landscapes dotted with chalets or small barns, some perched on stilts. It's also common to come across wayside cavalries set up to protect hikers and locals from the dark dangers of the mountains.

The old habits of isolation die hard in many villages. Many villagers are wary of strangers. Even if the woman from the next hamlet marries a man she will remain a stranger in his village for the rest of her life. Their children, however, are accepted on birth. The reason for this is that the peasants practiced an intense, largely self-sufficient mixed farming economy and they could ill-afford to share the paucity of their holdings with strangers. The key institution was the household and the extended family. Celibacy was common, households were constrained by the limit of resources. It was not unusual to find intermarriage and over a period of several hundred years, a predominance of people with the same family names appeared.

Culture
Music

The Valaisian valleys have always reverberated with music. On Sundays, you can hear the carillon of the church bells echoing along the valleys; on festival days the choirs sing and the brass bands play; and high up on the mountains you can hear the mournful sound of alphorns or joyful yodelling.

Over the years, the Church has played a significant role in music and the first known performance was in the Abbey of St Maurice (515 AD) where five choirs of

Carlen Organ, Reckingen Church.

monks, each in turn, sang the perpetual praise over a period of 24 hours. In Sion, on the top of Valere hill, there is the 13th century Notre Dame church that has the oldest organ in the world still in use.

By the end of the medieval period, there were many priories in the Valais spawning a tradition of singing. Today, choirs proliferate the villages and if you want to

socialise, it's best to join one. Brass bands are also popular and it's not unusual to find two or even three in some villages. In the Val d'Anniviers, there was a tradition for musicians to accompany whole villages down to Sierre to work on the vineyards in the summer.

The roots of Swiss folk music are based on the ancient customs of Alpine herdsmen of which the alphorn, yodelling and the Gregorian chant of the evening benediction or Alpsegen is part. The alphorn is about 9 ft long and when it's blown produces natural tones. Yodelling is a singing style characterised by frequent and rapid shifts from normal voice to falsetto and back again, interspersed with a few syllables like yo-lolo-dee-uuh. The Alpine shepherd chants a classical catholic litany in which he asks God, the Virgin Mary and various Saints for protection against danger. His voice is amplified by his all-purpose wooden funnel which he carries around with him.

The foundation of the Cantonal Conservatory of Music in Sion in 1947 has stimulated the interest in classical music. Part of the conservatory's responsibility has been to visit the various valleys to note the texts and melodies of old songs, some of which were brought back from France or Italy by mercenaries.

Every year in summer there are several music festivals. Sion has both the International Music festival and the Violin Competition. Ernen is well-known for its Piano Week, the Baroque Music Festival and the Festival of the Future. The programmes are always refreshing as the members of the orchestra do not belong

Alphorns at lake Tracouet.

to fixed groups but perform together as part of their music courses. Regular music events are also held at the Giannada Foundation, Martigny and La Poste, Visp. The resorts of Verbier, Saas-Fee and Zermatt also have annual events.

Art
Léonard Gianadda, Genius of Art

The Pierre Gianadda Foundation in Martigny is the major showcase for art. The Foundation has a sculpture garden and holds international exhibitions. Léonard Gianadda is the genius of culture in the Valais. What he has achieved since the establishment the Pierre Gianadda Foundation in 1978 is incredible. When his younger brother Pierre died as a result of a plane crash, Gianadda created a foundation in his memory. In the past three decades, he has mounted over 30

world-class exhibitions and musical events. Exhibitions have included Kees van Dongen, Bonnard, Turner, Manet, Gauguin, van Gogh, Picasso, among others, as well as showcasing collections from prominent museums like the Tretyakov Gallery, the Phillips Collection, the Metropolitan Museum of Art and the Pushkine Gallery. He has also focused on female artists such as Berthe Morisot and Frida Kahlo and Swiss artists like Albert Anker and Alberto Giacometti.

The sculpture park features 45 works that include Henry Moore and Rodin. You will also find at the Foundation, the Gallo-Roman ruins, a splendid automobile collection and an exhibition of Leonardo Da Vinci's inventions. In all, Gianadda has brought a veritable feast of international art to the Valais where, previously, the most popular form of culture was the cow fights. It was a big risk but he is not a man to balk at great challenges. "When you have something of quality," he said, "people will come from all over the world to see it." So far he has had almost 9 million visitors over the past 30 years, with an average of 700 a day.

Léonard Gianadda and Cecilia Bartoli.

Gianadda has consorted with British artists too. Dined with Francis Bacon and lunched with Lucian Freud, who turned up at the famous Colombe d'Or, St Paul de Vence, dressed in paint-splattered work clothes. The concerts at the Pierre Gianadda also have an international flavour with performers from the New York Opera and famous soloists like Murray Perahia, Daniel Barenboim and

Cecilia Bartoli. He is in awe of the diva whom he likens to singing like a bird when she vocalises Vivaldi's Agitata de due venti. He also has an anecdote about Isaac Stern. "When he played an encore at a concert, he turned his back to the audience and played it solely for Renoir's Venus. Utterly remarkable!" The concerts at the Foundation are renowned and usually have audiences of some 800 people.

A veritable Maecenas, Gianadda has donated many sculptures to Martigny, but has an uneasy relationship with the town. When the ruins of a Gallo-Roman temple were found on the site of the Foundation, he was angry when told to demolish it – now it's a big tourist attraction. He has been honoured with decorations from Italy, Russia and particularly France where he was made a Chevalier, Officier and Commander of the Légion d'honneur and an Academician of the Beaux-Arts. It took Martigny 30 years to award him a prize for culture. But then that is how the Valaisians treat its great sons like Stockalper and Gianadda.

What is surprising about Léonard Gianadda is that prior to the Foundation, he had a distinguished career as a reporter, cameraman and photographer. One of his first coups, was to photograph Georges Simenon, the Belgium author and creator of Inspector Maigret, who, in 1957, was on a visit to Lausanne. Simenon was so impressed with the results that his editor spent 5,000 CHF on the photos – equivalent then to an engineer's annual salary. He met his charming wife, Annette Pavid, in the same city, whose boss at Lausanne's Tourist Office also bought the Simenon photos. But in between this career and the establishment of the Foundation, Gianadda received a degree in civil engineering and for 15 years constructed over a 1,000 apartments in Martigny. And although he has never mentioned it, the accomplishment would have made his grandfather, Baptiste Gianadda, proud – a labourer who had walked all the way from Piedmont, Italy in order to find work on a Martigny building site because he was tired of hearing his parents crying that they did not have enough money to buy salt.

Esther Waeber-Kalbermatten with a Renato Jordan painting.

Esther Waeber-Kalbermatten is a Valaisian politician. When she was elected to office on the Statsrat, Sion, she bought her first painting from Renato Jordan. It was based on Rainer Maria Rilke's text "I see you, rose, half-open book..." (Rose poem II.) What appealed to her about Jordan's work was the tension between the text and the composition of the red and grey shapes. It is a double-layered work. One layer consists of all the signatures and the other the text of the declaration. The work stimulates reflection and hangs on the wall opposite her desk – when she looks up she sees it.

Waeber-Kalbermatten had come across Jordan's enormous decadal canvases at the United Nations Declaration of Human Rights in Geneva.

Literature

Rainer Maria Rilke (1875-1926), the German poet who was born in Prague, spent the last years of his life from 1921 to 1926 in Veyras, Sierre. It was there that he wrote his masterpieces, Duino Elegies and the Sonnets of Orpheus. When Rilke had first set eyes on the Valais, it had reminded him of Provence and Spain. "And this echo, this family likeness is not imaginary," he wrote to friends. "Only the other day, I read in a treatise on the plant world that certain flowers appear here which are otherwise found only in Provence and Spain. It's the same with the butterflies." It seemed to him that the spirit of the great river, the Rhone, carried such gifts and affinities through country after country.

But, what he desired most was an Elegy-place where he could be quiet, enjoy nature and solitude – he found it at an old tower called Muzot (pronounced 'Muzotte') whose walls dated back to the 13th century. "It lies some 20 minutes above Sierre, set pretty steeply in a less arid but happy countryside, gushing with many springs and with views of the valley, of the mountain slopes and far into the most marvellous depths of the sky."

By 1926, Rilke's health had deteriorated and he spent time at the Valmont clinic in Glion above Lake Geneva. But on his return, his illness made living in the little tower more difficult than in former days, so he lived alternately at the Hotel Bellevue in Sierre. (Now the town hall.) Another cycle of French poems, Orchards or Vergers, was published. They cheered him up and he added a cycle on Roses.

In October, he pricked two fingers while cutting the same flowers in his garden at Muzot. The cuts turned septic, began to suppurate and become intensely painful. It was soon apparent that these were symptoms of an acute leukemia. Rilke died early in the morning of Wednesday, December 29th, 1926. On Sunday, January 2nd, 1927, four men carried the coffin up the steep icy footpath to the Burgkirche in Raron while in front of them walked the local magistrate with a wooden cross. After the service, according to local custom, children formed a circle around the open grave. They held up heavy wreaths, their hands blue with cold during the stranger's interment. Not a soul in Raron knew the poet, yet reverence surrounded him. Rilke is buried in the graveyard beside the old Burgkirche on the hill in Raron. It was there that he had first espied the Valaisian landscape.

Katherine Mansfield. Katherine Mansfield Beauchamp Murray (1888-1923) was born into a prominent colonial family in Wellington, New Zealand. At the age of 18, she went to England where she fell in love with a young musician, became pregnant and rashly married her singing teacher – all within seven months of her arrival. She had courage and talent and became one of the best short story writers of her period. She was deeply disappointed by her family and friends and her weak and selfish husband, John Middleton Murray. Yet, she understood him and even mooted the idea that he should divorce her as she would never be a wife to him and marry a healthy, young creature and have children. He betrayed her with her close friend, Dorothy Brett, and couldn't help her when she was dying because she insisted that she had to discover her true self on her own. Her "desire to learn to work in the right way and to live as a conscious human being."

During the last years of her life (1921 to 1922) she lived for periods in Montana-sur-Sierre. By New Year 1922, Katherine Mansfield and her husband had been at the Chalet des Sapins for almost six months. Some of her best stories were written during that time, At the Bay, The Garden Party, The Voyage and the uncompleted A Man's Story. But, life in the chalet was isolated and the winter months severe. Sometimes, 7 ft of snow would lie outside their door and in her letters she would either rail against the snow or be comforted by it. In a letter to her husband's brother (January 2nd, 1922) she wrote: "Yes, the snow is terrific. It is like living on the moon. Trees are crashing to the earth and lamp posts are falling and there is no electric light, no little mountain railway!"

Mansfield had come to the Valais following a diagnosis of tuberculosis in 1917. She decided to spend the English winters abroad and, in her last years, to seek unorthodox cures. Her father, a wealthy banker who gave her a regular allowance, would not pay for expensive tuberculosis treatments and anyway, she rejected the idea of a sanatorium as such a confinement would cut her off from writing.

In February, 1922, she left for Paris to undertake the revolutionary treatment of the Russian physician, Ivan Manoukhine. It consisted of bombarding her spleen with x-rays which caused her to be "hotted up inside like a furnace and one's very bones seem to be melting." Manoukhine had first assured her that she had no cavities in her lungs which meant that she was curable. But, a disbelief held her back about the treatment's effectiveness. She was confident but she was divided. Her instincts finally proved right and the dark secret unbelief won over. She became terribly ill and the treatment weakened her heart.

Mansfield returned to Montana-sur-Sierre for three months and then again made a trip to London before she surrendered herself to the mystic George Gurdjieff at his institute outside Paris. It was in a beautiful old chateau which was formerly a Carmelite monastery and she joined a colony of some 50 people, mainly Russians. Everyone was working at every kind of possible thing. There was outdoor work, animal husbandry, gardening, indoor work, music and dancing. And Mansfield made up her mind to live by what she believed in. Up until then, she had felt disunited as she had lived one way and thought another. During the first week of the new year, she already found signs of spring. There were Christmas roses under the Espalier pear trees which reminded her of Switzerland. When her husband came to visit her on January 9th, 1923 she ran upstairs to show him how well she was and died of a fatal pulmonary haemorrhage later that evening. She was only 34.

Stéphanie Corinna Bille (known as S. Corinna Bille) was a writer who won the Prix Goncourt in 1975 for a short story. As such she was quite a phenomenon in the peasant culture of the Valais where in ancient times people would tie corpses to mules to take them across the mountains.

Bille was the eldest daughter of the Swiss artist Edmond Bille and his second wife, Catherine Tapparel. Her childhood was spent in her father's Baroque mansion overlooking Sierre. Her father was a painter, engraver and stained glass artist and became renowned for his stained glass windows in various churches like the Abbaye in St Maurice and the Town Hall in Martigny – where he created the largest stained glass window in Switzerland. Bille assisted her father in the studio and posed for him. He guided her first attempts at writing and by the age of 16, she vowed to become a writer, collecting material for her work from the local newspaper and from her mother's peasant relatives in the villages, Corin and Lower Corin near Sierre. One of her short stories, The Grape Harvest, tells of a seasonal labourer on the vineyards, a young woman who like most of her characters was an outsider. In spite of her success, little of Bille's life and work has been published in English.

Death's cheese.

A Wacky List

Isolated and protected by the Alps, the Valais has always been a strange Canton. Below is a list of its many idiosyncrasies:

1. Death's cheese, glacier wine and a table for the dead

The Val d'Anniviers is a most unusual place and there are many strange customs. The most important event in a person's life is the celebration of their death. On their marriage, a large cheese is set aside which will be eaten on the day of their funeral. Originally poor, they wanted to ensure that their relatives and friends had something to eat on their death, at their funeral. But by then the cheese was so hard that slices had to be sawn off.

Glacier wine is kept in the cellar of the Maison de la Bourgeoisie in Grimentz. Another oddity, it is at least 125 years old and originates from the white grape variety, rèze. The wine is self-sustaining and whenever the barrel reaches the halfway mark, it is topped up with the new vintage. The wine from the 1888 barrel tops up the 1886 barrel and the 1934 refills the 1888, while the 1969 which replenishes the 1934 will receive the new wine. Moniseur Jean Vouardoux, who is the master of ceremonies in Grimentz, is in charge of wine tasting. You are given a small glass and a thin sliver of 50-year-old death's cheese. The glacier wine tastes like sherry. Afterwards, he opens the visitor's book to show a photo of himself and Cherie Blair! On a tour of the house you are taken into the hall which is decorated with several rows of silver and pewter tankards on the wall. Each was a gift from the villagers over the past three hundred years. The room has several tables

Jean Vouardoux with Glacier wine.

reserved for specific groups. The largest is for members of the council; another is for those doing community jobs; three are for villagers according to their age; and the last one is for the 'dead' – old men who can no longer work and therefore are designated the 'dead' of the community.

2. The Mountain Ridges Train or Gratzug
There is a legend in the Upper Valais that the sinners never come to rest. They are condemned to return to the place where they committed the treachery. These crimes could be little transgressions like dancing or working on Sunday. The sinners live on the glaciers and twice a year join the ghost train that runs along the ridges of the mountains. If you are out at night on November 2nd, All Souls day, or on January 14th, St Hilary of Poitier's feast day, you might see the poor souls.

Should you meet the eyes of the last one in the procession, you could save them if you say, "I'll give you part of my breath, but the first and the last word is mine." But you must speak of God at the beginning.

3. Cholera
Cholera is neither the disease nor an antidote to it. It's a pie found in the Goms valley and is made from raclette cheese, onions, leek, potatoes, pears and apples and a strip of thin bacon or petit lard. It originated during an outbreak of cholera in the 1830's when it was safer to stay indoors and live off food you normally kept in your cellar. Recipes are passed from mother to daughter and are jealously guarded.

4. Albinen's Ladders
The shortest route to Leukerbad for the

people in Albinen was to scale a cliff face 328 ft high via ladders. There were eight ladders of various sizes placed at different levels which enabled you to ascend or descend with produce or animals carried on your back. But you had to have a head for heights!

5. The Blackneck Goat

The forequarters of the blackneck goat are black while the hindquarters are white. The hair is long and wavy and the medium-length horns are arched. It has never been quite established whether the origins of this ancient Valaisian species can be traced back to Africa or if they are descended from the Italian 'Kupferziege' goats. Originally, they were mostly found in the Lower Valais and almost became an extinct breed. Now the 'glacier goat' is protected by the Pro Specie Rara organisation.

6. The Blacknosed Sheep

The breed originates in the Valais and was first mentioned in 1400. The blacknosed sheep is a docile mountain species which was first recognised in 1962. It has adapted particularly well to life at high altitude and grazes even on the steepest, stoniest slopes. It has black patches on its nose, eyes, ears, knees, hocks and feet. The wool is coarse and both rams and ewes have horns.

Wine

"If you dig deep enough you will find that most people in the Valais have some connection with wine production."
Claude-Alain Margelisch, Chief Executive Officer, Swiss Bankers Association

The Valais is the most famous wine growing region in Switzerland. What sets it apart from the rest of the wine world is

Cornalin.

Blacknosed sheep.

the terroir and the unusual grape varieties which can titillate the palate in unfamiliar ways. A remarkable feature of the Valais is the extraordinary mixture of soil types, sun exposure and microclimate. You find the old native varieties which are unknown elsewhere such as Amigne, Arvine, Cornalin, Humagne and Rèze. Vines are grown along a 50 mile strip of the Rhône valley, mainly on the sunny steep slopes of the south facing Bernese Alps which extends from Martigny to Brig. It's a glacial valley with a relatively flat floor and some vineyards are on slopes as steep as 70°. The construction and maintenance of these are labour intensive and hence, costly. Much wine here is grown at high altitudes from around 2,132 ft to 3,772 ft at Visperterminen in the Upper Valais – one of the highest in Europe. The Valais is characterised by the presence of 59 grape varieties with 26 red and 33 white. However, three varieties such as Fendant, Pinot Noir and Gamay alone account for over 70% of the growing area. The powerful reds from indigenous and international grape varieties rival anything produced elsewhere in Europe, and a range of whites which are among the great sweet wines of Europe.

The first traces of viticulture appeared in the Valais even before the Roman era but viticulture really got underway in the Middle Ages. By 1300, the vineyards of the upper Rhone valley already had the dimensions that corresponded with those known in the second half of the 19th century. The cultivation of the vineyards was in the hands of peasant families who paid an annual rent to the landowners. Wine was considered to be a food and its production was essentially to satisfy the needs of the family or the congregation during the year. Commercial exchanges were unknown. It was only towards the end of the Middle Ages around, 1500, that wine was bought and sold.

The commercial development of the wine growing industry began in 1850 after the civil war, the Sonderbund (1847), when the plundered properties were bought by wealthy Valaisian families and by investors from the canton of Vaud who created the first wine businesses. There were two other factors which stimulated the growth of the industry. The containment of the Rhone which freed up land for viticulture and the construction of the railways that opened up new commercial opportunities. Wine became the most important crop in Valaisian agriculture.

During the 1920s, wine growers could not make a living from their vineyards and the first cooperative Provins was founded. The Federal government played a greater role in the industry and introduced oenological studies for the peasants so that a professional level could be attained. By 1957, the Valais was the top wine growing canton in Switzerland. More and more land was turned over to cultivation of vineyards and the record level of 3,550 hectares was reached in 1980. This led to a serious crisis of overproduction and the bottom fell out of the market. A change in direction was necessary and quality took precedence over quantity. To ensure that there was an increase in the quality of wines, the AOC (appellation d'origine contrôlée) certificate was established and enabled checks to be carried out in the vineyards. Native varieties were re-introduced, the quality of soils improved and the safeguard of the scenic landscape were set as goals of the wine growing policy.

Containing the Rhone by Raphael Ritz 1888.

To encourage visitors to get to know Valais wines, the winegrowers have created 'the wine route' which runs from Martigny to Leuk. It's some 41 miles long and consists mostly of nature trails which vary from 1,476-2,624 ft. The route has been chosen with care so that it can easily be walked, biked or driven and is lined with restaurants and vineyards where you can taste wine.

Guerite of Maurice Gay for workers and equipment.

A view of Sion.

A walk along 'the wine route'.

Wine Growers

There are many outstanding wineries in the Valais and in fact you are spoilt for choice. However, I have selected two exemplars, Marie-Thérèse Chappaz and Diego Mathier.

Marie-Thérèse Chappaz.

Queen of Valaisian Wine.

Marie-Thérèse Chappaz was introduced to vintages as a child when she sipped wine from her father Claude's spoon. His wine cellar was filled with the best wines and she remembers decanting the premier Côtes de Bordeaux from the barrel into bottles. She liked the very tannic taste unlike the Valaisian reds which are easier on the palate. Although her father always wanted her to become a winegrower she resisted at first and became a midwife. But, when at the age of 18 he gave her a small vineyard in Charrat, she decided to try her hand at viniculture and soon found that she liked the outdoor life better than the indoor life of a hospital. She trained as an oenologist at Changins and later, worked at the research centre in Fribourg.

As a winemaker of over two decades, she now nurtures vines to birth their best in the environment of biodynamic agriculture in 14 hectares of vineyards. Her steep slopes are covered with weeds and wild plants like marjoram, oregano, hyssop, St John's wort and thyme. Her speciality is the sweet noble rot wines which are made from petite arvine grapes that are covered with a beneficial form of grey fungus, botrytis cinerea. She decries the activities of others who pander to the tastes of consumers. "It's a dangerous course to take," she says, "to add shavings and aromas. The wine should be an expression of the Valais. It should reflect the grape variety, the terroir, the climate, the area and the mettre en valeur."

The consumers, too, have to take their role seriously. "They should not drink something they don't like, it's not etiquette. Train your palate, take time to taste," she said. "Find something you like. The wine speaks, listen to what it says. Above all, it provokes an emotion."

She arranged a wine tasting for me at her home. Present were cheeses like Tomme, Vacherin Fribourgeois, Bagnes, Brillat Saverin, Stilton and Gruyère. There were only two wines, Grain Noble (2006), a noble rot wine, and a Dôle de la Liaudisaz. The purpose was to find an explosion between the cheese and the wine. Put in another way, it was to find the perfect marriage between the two, where the combination brings out the best in the wine and the cheese. We first tried the Grain Noble or Marsanne Blanche, which was a thick nectar unlike any other sweet wine I've ever tasted. It's distinguished by aromas of rhubarb, wisteria, violet, grapefruit and lychee.

The Tomme was too young; the Vacherin Fribourgeois was a month too old; the Gruyère brought the worst out in the wine; the Bagnes which on a previous occasion had caused an explosion, just did not perform; and the Stilton, which was the best match, was too grainy in texture and not creamy enough. The cherry red Dôle, which had a darkness and depth with aromas of myrtle and cassis was not happy with the choice of cheeses.

La Liaudisaz, Fully is a good place to stop and taste Madame Chappaz's biological range of whites and reds. For those who like Beaujolais, try her Gamay of which she has seven Grand Cru. For a superb red, the Grain Mariage, a mixture of Cornalin and Humagne Rouge which has an aroma of damp forest and deep cherry. The Grain Cornalin has an aroma of toast and has a sensual animal aftertaste. A last word about the Marsanne Blanc – it's silky with a complex palate that can accompany most dishes from delicate poultry to strong Breton lobsters.

Diego Mathier.

The Crown Prince of Valasian Wine

When Diego Mathier one day realises his vision of the perfect vintage, he will become the king. Already, he is on the right track – it's paved with hundreds of gold and silver medals from both international and Swiss competitions. He will do it on his own terms because, as he says, "I'm the biggest critic of my own wines." He learnt about criticism at first hand when he asked the aristocrats of the great wines of Bordeaux to comment on his vintages. Now, after ten grape harvests, he admits that he's only beginning to understand what perfect wines are all about. He tells you that it took him four years to be calibrated on the same scale with Cédric Leyat, his oenologist.

Diego is the fourth generation of winemakers in Salgesch and he remembers with pride when, on his sixth birthday, his parents served sweet wine at his party for his thirteen young guests. He describes himself as a gourmet, or gniesser in the local patois, who enjoys good food and wine. Then he admits that he has some 7,000 bottles of wine in his private cellar.

Our wine tasting takes place in his vast cellar because he likes to move around the big stainless steel vats and heaped oak barrels where maceration and alcoholic fermentation occur. It's an inspiration to be present, in his own words: "The future is in the barrel." I'm eager to taste his wines which are approaching the peak of perfection. He is armed with three wine glasses as Leyat will join us. We start with the whites – Chasselas, Petite Arvine, Marsanne (dry) and Chardonnay, and then move on to the reds. What I find is that all his wines have a good balance that he describes as the backbone of vintages. But it's the charisma and character that can be elusive. If there are wines that are high on Diego's percentage scale, it's the Ambassador des Domaines Diego Mathier (Pinot Noir) which is 90%, the red Folissimo which is 90-92%, the Gemma Ermitage Smaragd which is 90% and lastly, Petite Arvine de Molignon which is 88%.

When it comes to the accompaniment to his wines, Diego is an iconoclast. He breaks the rules! A wine like Pinot Noir which is the gentleman of reds can be drunk with fish. A Gamay with raclette. It would be remiss not to mention other members of his family who are also experienced winemakers. His mother Rosmarie whose Cuvée rouge and Cuvée white won awards and his wife, Nadia's superb Merlot. The winery, Adrian Mathier, in Salgesch (or Salquenen in French) is a must for any connoisseur as is the village which is renowned for its vintages.

Irrigation in the Valais

There are over 200 watercourses ('bisse' in French, 'suonen' in German) in the Valais which funnel the glacial waters

along the mountain slopes. When a rocky wall blocks their path, they run through wooden troughs suspended over vertiginous drops. The maintenance of the bisses and the careful distribution of their water plays an essential role in the lives of the peasants in the small mountain communities. Their water supply is supplemented by six of the tallest and highest dams in the world.

Nendaz, in the region of Sion, has the largest network in Europe – eight man-made watercourses run on terraces at altitudes of between 2,624 ft and 7,217 ft. The Bisse de Salins, which dates from 1435, is the oldest in the commune and provides water for the meadows, orchards and crops of three villages including Salins. The route travels through a forest, over a metal footbridge (which is suspended over the torrent of

Ojintse) and then into a large meadow. The bisses vary in length and include the longest – the Saxon at 21 miles and the

Baar, which has a magnificent view over the Rhône valley and irrigates apricot orchards for which Nendaz is well-known.

Mountaineering

The Golden Age of mountaineering began with the founding of the Alpine Club, London, in 1857, and within a short period of eight years until 1865, the vast majority of the great alpine peaks were conquered. It was an epoch that was to culminate in the ascent by Edward Whymper of the most striking and the most inaccessible of them all, the Matterhorn, in the Valais.

The members of the Alpine Club were predominently graduates of Oxford and Cambridge and belonged to the professions that demanded intellectual qualities such as university dons, civil servants, lawyers, clergymen and diplomats. An exception was Charles

Suonen of Baltschiedertal.

Barrington, an all-round sportsman and jockey, who on his first visit to Switzerland and with no experience of mountaineering, climbed the 13,025-ft Eiger in the Bernese Alps. His party set off in the evening and at 3 am they were on the slopes. His plan was to tackle the north-west face, whose cliffs appeared precipitous. Later, when they were confronted by an exceedingly steep, rocky climb, the guides declared the route impossible. "I said I would try," he wrote to his brother afterwards. "So with the rope coiled over my shoulders, I scrambled up, sticking like a cat to the rocks, which cut my fingers and at last got up say, 50 or 60 feet. I lowered the rope and the guides followed with its assistance." By noon, Barrington was proudly planting a British flag on the Eiger's summit and by early evening, he

had returned to the Wengern Alp hotel. The hotel owner fired off a large gun and he was lionized that evening. The insouciant Barrington capped his ascent of the Eiger with, "Thus ended my first and only visit to Switzerland."

Sir Leslie Stephen, father of Virginia Woolf, was another intrepid mountaineer and his enquiring mind was matched by athletic prowess. He was a Cambridge man who thought nothing of walking the 60 miles to London for dinner and then back the next day. If you could walk horizontally, he had reasoned, why not vertically. Between 1858 and 1871, he conquered nine peaks including the 12,021 ft. Blümlisalphorn in the Bernese Oberland, the nearby 13,375 ft Schreckhorn, the 13,848 ft Zinalrothorn and the rocky 12,900 ft Bietschhorn. He

Mont Blanc Massif from the Clochetons of Pierre Avoi.

once said of the Jungfrau Pass that it was "a pass which cannot be climbed, so we have to do it."

The list of the conquerors of the Valasian Alps is endless: In 1861, Professor John Tyndall mastered one of the highest peaks, the 14,780 ft Weisshorn and one of the most beautiful; J.C. Davies climbed the nearby 14,757-ft Täschhorn; Thomas Stuart Kennedy had beaten the 14,295-ft Dent Blanche, a few miles west; and D.C. McDonald and F.C. Grove conquered the 13,684-ft Dent d'Hérens, to the west of the Matterhorn. But the biggest prize was taken by a young engraver, Edward Whymper, who at the age of 25 was an experienced climber.

Towering over the village of Zermatt at the head of St Nicholas valley, the 14,780-ft Matterhorn was the last great alpine peak which remained unscaled. It was reputed by the locals to be inhabited by demons, dragons in fact, who would resist all human approaches. As the leader of the expedition, Whymper wrote, "There seemed to be a cordon drawn around it, up to which one might go but no farther." The guides also discouraged him, "Anything but Matterhorn, dear sir! Anything but Matterhorn."

Whymper reached the summit, writing: "At 1.40 pm the world was at our feet and the Matterhorn was conquered! Hurrah! Not a footstep could be seen." But tragedy would mar the expedition. Four members of his team died on the descent, making headline news throughout Europe.

The Regions

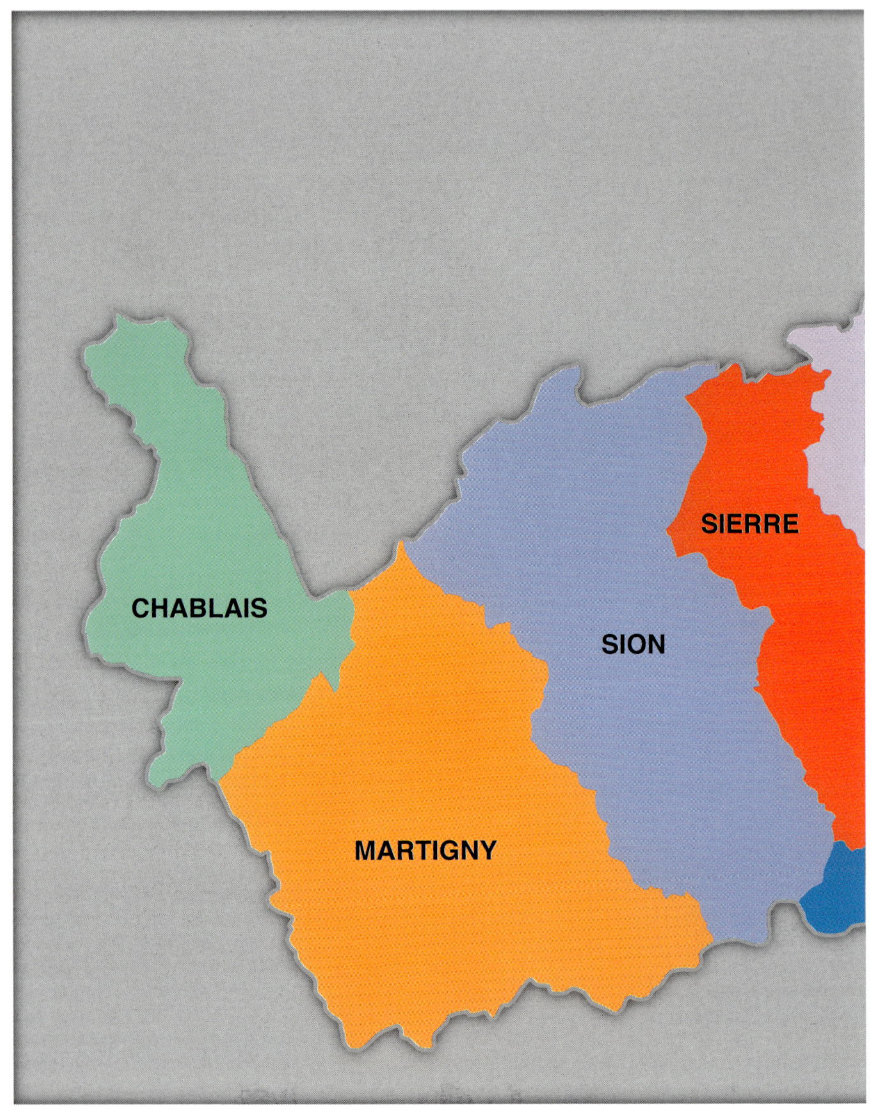

The Regions

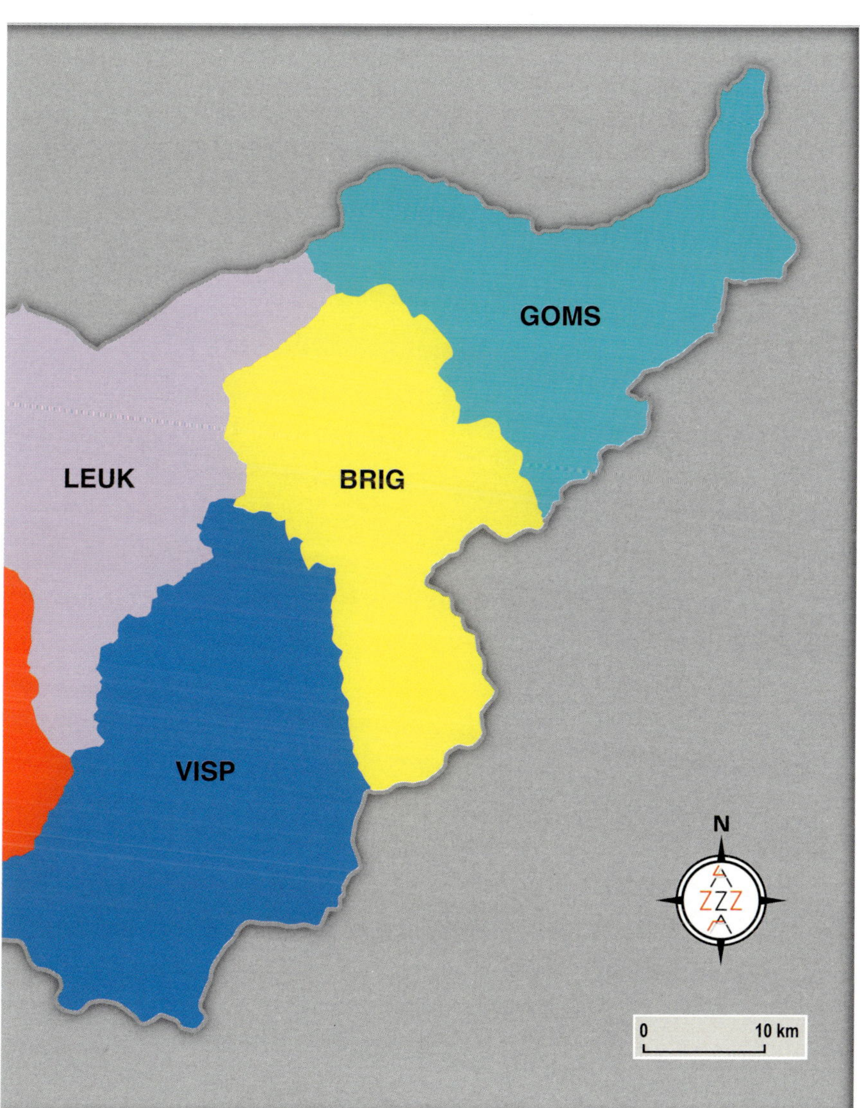

RHÔNE GLACIER AND ICE GROTTO - ALETSCH ARENA

BAROQUE CHURCHES - MINERALS FROM THE BINN VALLEY

HIKING AND SKIING - RESTAURANTS

THE 9-MILE SLED RUN - FURKA STEAM TRAIN

Chapter 2: The Regions

Goms

At a glance

Rhône glacier and ice grotto

A famous visitor who walked on the glacier was Queen Victoria. She was accompanied by her daughter Princess Louise who also went inside the ice grotto. The road to the glacier and ice grotto is open from June to the middle of October. Both are a 15-minute walk from the Belvedere hotel. For further information ring 027 924 3824.

Aletsch Arena

A natural wonder that should not be missed on any visit to the Valais. The mammoth ice sheet is the longest in the Alps and winds its way down from the base of the Jungfrau. The finest view of this UNESCO World Natural Heritage site is from Fiesch with the cable car up to Eggishorn.

Baroque Churches

Some 70 churches and chapels line the 31-mile long valley. Reckingen with its 18th century Carlen organ, Münster with the Gothic triptych and Ernen's St George are recommended.

Minerals from the Binn Valley

Goms is one of the richest mineral sites in the world – some of which are unique to the area. Hikers can find a wide range of colourful stones and glittering quartz crystals. All you need is a special hammer that can be obtained from the Kiosk at Feld just outside Binn. Souvenir minerals are also available in local shops.

Tourist office

Tel. 027 971 4547.

Hiking and Skiing

In summer, Goms is a paradise for hiking with 434 miles of trails over mountains, passes and glaciers. Mountain bikers have 186 miles of signposted routes and paths. In winter, heavy snowfall ensures the best cross-country skiing in the Valais.

Restaurants

Niederwald is the birthplace of César Ritz, the pioneer of luxury hotels and dining. The tradition has been maintained by restaurants in the region offering Ritzy menus. Among those are the Ahorni (Oberwald), Baschi (Geschinen), Mühle (Geschinen), Croix d'Or et Poste (Münster), Landhaus (Münster), Blinnenhorn (Reckingen), Hotel Glocke (Reckingen), Tenne (Gluringen), Castle (Blitzingen), Drei Tannen (Niederwald), Ambassador (Bellwald), St George (Ernen), Gommerstube (Niederernen) and

Goms

Jägerheim (Ausserbinn). A booklet that includes a recipe for Goms Cholera can be obtained from the Tourist Office in Fiesch. For more information: Tel 027 970 1070

The 9-mile Sled Run

The longest sled run in the Valais is from Fiescheralp down to Lax and Fiesch.

The Furka Steam Train

The Furka cogwheel steam railway, open from June to the beginning of October, runs between Gletsch and Realp in Canton Uri. Dampfbahn Furka-Bergstrecke AG Tel. 0848 000 144 www.furka-bergstrecke.ch/eng

Tourist Offices Goms.

Welcome Center Ernen
CH-3995 Ernen
Tel. 027 971 17 42
www.ernen.ch

Eggishorn Tourismus
CH-3984 Fiesch
Tel. 027 970 60 70
www.eggishorn.ch
mail to: info@fiesch.ch

Bellwald Tourismus
CH-3997 Bellwald
Tel. 027 971 16 84
www.bellwald.ch

Gästecenter Obergoms
CH-3985 Münster
Tel. 027 974 68 68
www.obergoms.ch

It's fitting to begin with Goms because the source of the great river Rhône that flows west into Lake Geneva, lies at the hamlet of Gletsch. It's fed by a glacier of the same name and the village is at the junction of roads from the Furka Pass, the Grimsel Pass, the lower valley and Nufenen Pass. Higher up on the Furka road where the Hotel Belvedere stands, you will find the Rhône Glacier in which an ice grotto has been carved out as well as a sweeping panorama of the Bernese and Valaisian Alps.

Queen Victoria, who made a private and secret visit to Switzerland in 1868, came to see the Rhône Glacier on the afternoon of August 24th, 1868. She was accompanied by her daughter, Princess Louise, and had spent the night at the Furka inn. The visit was recorded in her diary. "We gazed with wonder & astonishment at the splendid glacier. When we got down, we found 2 horses quietly waiting, which the coachman (a careful good driver) fastened on behind our carriage & thus we trotted on, quite to the foot of the glacier, where the Rhone runs out from underneath it, in a thick white stream. Went up to the Hotel du Rhone Glacier, where a good many people seemed to be stopping. Here, we had to get out, however we got on as quickly as we could, & Alpenstock in hand, walked about ½ a mile along a path, crossing a little stream over rough stones, till we came to the glacier itself where it was level. With the help of Brown & Hoffmann I walked a little way on it & back. It cracked a little, but the thickness of the ice is quite enormous. It looks brown & rather dirty. Louise then went to a cavern with Sir T. Biddulph,

Source of the Rhône.

Rhône glacier.

which is scooped out in the ice a good long way. I walked slowly back to where Hoffmann had kindled a fire, & where we sat on the grass under a small bank, watching the water boil in a casserole, a kettle being unknown in these parts. Had some delicious tea, then hurried off to our carriage, to which 4 horses were now attached. Went off in grand style, the whip being well smacked & the good little horses encouraged by that peculiar 'hau-ip', which the men here constantly call to them. On the level we got on fast, then came that tremendous long ascent of certainly 1000 ft, which took us 5 quarters of an hour to accomplish. We met men who go up daily to milk the cows, & carry milk & butter, even cheese, on their backs. Often these are conveyed in small carts, drawn by poor dogs. The moon shone out over the glacier, as we were driving back & it & the mountains looked too beautiful. Hoffmann & the driver yodelled as we went along. Got in at 1/2p. 7.″

By 1907, the glacier had retreated and it took half an hour by path to reach it. At the back of the Hotel du Rhône there were three tepid springs that were regarded as the source of the Rhône. Nowadays, there's a gentle walk of half an hour from

Reckingen church (above).

Münster church (below).

Gletsch to reach the source which is behind a smooth lump of rock.

In 1925 the mountain of the steam train was built and today visitors can experience nostalgia by sitting in the original carriages pulled by the old locomotives. The journey begins at Realp in Canton Uri (1,420m above sea level) First, the old steam engine climbs uphill along the Furkareuss river, crosses the Wiler bridge, through three tunnels and across the Steffenbach folding bridge. The locomotive is filled up with water at the first stop in Tiefenbach. Then the train crosses the Steinstafel viaduct before a short halt is made at the highest station, Furka (2160m). From there it enters the mile long tunnel before a stop at Muttbach-Belvédère. The descent into Valais begins with a gradient up to 118 pro mille. Soon, the Rhone Glacier comes into view

The climate in Goms lends itself to heavy snowfalls and the region has the best cross-country skiing in the Valais. The ski areas of Bellwald, Erner Galen and Fiescheralp-Eggishorn, along the edge of the Aletsch Glacier, offer mixed slopes for every level of ability. There are also over 434 miles of hiking trails over mountains, passes and glaciers and mountain bikers have 186 miles of signposted routes and paths.

The village of Ernen which was once the capital of Goms, has an ancient history as it dates back to the second Iron Age and to the Roman era. Ernen is a jewel among its peers not only because of its musical festival but of the concentration of outstanding buildings in this village.

There is the church of St George, the Jost-Sigristen house (1581) with its torture chamber, the House of Goms Dizain (1762) and William Tell house (1576) both of which are found in Hengert Square or as it's known in Swiss-German dialect, 'chatting square'.

The church of St George was built in the 16th century on the foundation of an 11th-century Roman basilica by the master builder Ulrich Ruffiner – renowned for his buildings in the Valais. The altar is a perfect example of the Rococo style with its ornamental intertwining asymmetrical patterns that feature motifs covered by gold lichen-like ornaments. Of particular note is the wooden sculpture of the Pieta which is a copy of the oldest in Switzerland (circa 1350). The organ (1679) is placed high up near the ceiling with a light source from a single window. It was built by the famous Aebi and restored by the well-known organist Felix Carlen (1792).

There's an additional bonus in visiting Ernen because of its proximity to the hamlet of Binn and the ancient cluster of Pagan wooden houses in nearby Mühlebach – the birthplace of Cardinal Mathew Schiner. Binn has an ancient necropolis, an archeological museum with displays of minerals and prehistoric artefacts and is served by a Belle Epoque hotel, the Offenhorn, which is being lovingly restored by the locals. It is also the centre of one of the largest mineral deposits in the world. The unspoilt nature reserve of Binn valley which surrounds Binn is a haven for mineralogists worldwide as it has over 200 types of crystals and minerals. Some varieties are rare like Wallisite and Binnite as well as 25 other world exclusives. Visitors can rent a hammer and box and collect their own specimens.

The nature reserve is also interesting because of the flora and fauna and its several lakes. One of the most beautiful, and easily accessible, is set amid moorland

William Tell Housem, Ernen.

Binn bridge.

Binn Valley.

Cardinal Schiner.

of national importance. The Schaplersee is in the middle of lush alpine meadows and at 7,874 ft is the Geisspfadsee, a series of glacial lakes in a bleak scree landscape.

But the jewel of them all is the Blausee or Grengjer See which is on a terrace in the Saflisch valley.

Hanging bridge, Aletsch.

Sightseeing in and around Goms

Aletsch Arena

The Aletsch Arena is a vast natural stadium in which to view the mammoth ice sheet that covers 45 square miles and is the longest in the Alps. The glacier is in the Bernese Alps and stretches from Belalp to the Lötschen Valley. Glacier comes from the Latin word for ice and glaciers are great rivers of ice. They are the largest reservoirs of fresh water on earth and store it in one season, only to release it the next as melt water. When you hear the loud sound of torrents in the mountains and see water gushing along the irrigation systems in the summer, this is what is happening. A glacier flows slowly due to the stresses induced by its immense weight. The consequence of its flow is the transport of rock and debris

Aletsch glacier.

and over time, it carves out land forms like cirques and moraines. Crevasses form when there are differences in the speed of various glacier areas and sections break apart. Since 1850, the glaciers have retreated worldwide and alpine glaciers, which are typically smaller and less stable, seem to be susceptible to glacial retreat. The Aletsch Glacier has retreated slightly and some thinning can be seen. It moves at a rate of 180 metres a year.

Spectacular views of the Aletsch Glacier can be obtained from the cable cars that travel from Mörel to Riederalp and from Betten to Bettmeralp. Both these car-free resorts, perched on the ridge-top plateaus, have lifts that serve the huge and unspoilt Aletsch forest nature reserve that overlooks this UNESCO World Natural Heritage site. But the finest view of the Aletsch Glacier is from the cable car from Fiesch up to the Eggishorn. The first stage takes you up over a spruce forest and scree of greenish-coloured jagged rocks. From the upper station (9,412 ft), there is a superb panorama. Below in the immediate foreground is the Aletsch Glacier, the Fiesch Glacier and a nearby cascade further round to the right of all the other neighbouring mountain peaks. For an even

Bettmeralp chalets.

Sled run, Lax to Fiesch.

Villa Cassel.

wider view, climb to the top of one of the three mounds of scree close to the upper station. The Eggishorn summit is marked by a cross.

The sunny plateau of the Aletsch Arena is one of the fortunate places in that you can step out of the chalet or hotel directly onto the ski slopes from December to April. Riederalp, Bettmeralp and Fiescheralp offer 62 miles of pistes including beginner slopes, snow parks and free-ride pistes. There's even an ice rink in Bettmeralp and an eight-mile sledding run from Fiescheralp down to Lax in the valley. In the summer, you can hike in the Aletsch forest and see the abundance of flora and fauna. There are some 93 miles of well-marked hiking trails which feature fixed-rope climbing routes and a 406 ft suspension bridge. But a big bonus

is that while temperatures climb in the valley, you can still be cool on the Aletsch plateaus (6,578 ft).

Another area to explore is around Riederfurka where a British banker built the Villa Cassel in 1902 and entertained Sir Winston Churchill. There you can find the Centre Pro Natura with a natural science exhibition and an Alpine Garden.

BAROQUE CASTLE OF THE THREE KINGS

STOCKALPER TOWER HOTEL - GONDO GORGE

SIMPLON DORF - EAGLE SCULPTURE

GANTER BRIDGE - THE VIA STOCKALPER

The Regions

Brig

At a glance

Baroque Castle of the Three Kings

Built by Kaspar Stockalper, the castle in the town of Brig has a large garden. There are guided tours through the great hall to view its original 17th-century panelling, the castle museum and the chapel.

Stockalper Tower hotel

The historic hotel has a Goldmine museum and is in the village of Gondo.

Gondo Gorge

Gondo gorge inspired the poet William Wordsworth to write the Prelude.

Simplon Dorf

There are three good reasons for breaking your journey over the pass. The bijoux Ecomuseum, the Tearoom bakery Arnold with its unusual confisserie, and the cheesemonger Sennerei whose cheeses are so good that Italians cross the border to buy them even although they're more expensive than those back in Italy.

Simplon Pass Eagle

The Eagle near the Simplon-Blick hotel/restaurant looks south in a threatening manner towards Italy. It was built in 1944 and has been compared to the ancient Egyptian stone statues of the Colossi of Memnon.

Ganter Bridge

Ganter bridge is made from reinforced concrete and is the longest spanning bridge in Switzerland. It's at an elevation of 4,760 ft above the Ganter river and six miles south of Brig. Designed by Christian Menn, it was a favourite for suicides until the high fence was erected.

The via Stockalper

The via Stockalper is one of the cultural routes of Switzerland. It follows the mule track from Brig to Gondo. The 19-mile route can be done in three stages. Brig to Simplon pass, Simplon pass to Simplon Dorf and Simplon Dorf to Gondo. See www.wanderland.ch or www.simplon.ch for further details. If you fancy brunch on the way you can stop just after the Altes Spittel on the r.h.s from the Brig direction or ring 027 9791318 or 079 606 1318

Hiking and Skiing

Hike over 62 miles of trails with the difference that you can walk in a circumference. In the winter, there is cross-country skiing, ice climbing and snowkiting on the Simplon pass.

Tourist Offices

Simplon Dorf and Gondo
Tel. 027 979 10 10
www.simplon.ch
Open: 16-31 August daily. 1 pm – 5 pm.
From 1-15 June and 1 September-31
October, Wednesday to Sunday 1 pm to
5 pm.

Brig Belalp Tourist Office
At Brig station.
Tel. 027 921 60 30
www.brig-belalp.ch

Brig is at the junction of the road to Goms
and the Rhône glacier, and the Simplon
road. It's also at the north end of the
Simplon tunnel, one of the longest rail
tunnels in the world. The main attraction
in the town of Brig is the Stockalper
castle which was once the largest private
residence in Switzerland. It can be
recognised from a distance by its three
bulbous towers.

The Simplon Pass (6,578 ft) links
Switzerland to the south through Italy
and is an ancient pass that was used by
armies, traders and pilgrims over the
past 2,000 years. There are traces of
the Romans through the epigraphs and
coins found along the route. But mostly
it was favoured by the merchants. In
the second half of the 16th century, the
pass was divided into three sections with
warehouses or Sustens from which they
sold goods and animals. The villages of
Brig, Simplon, Gondo and in Italy, Varza,
which along the route were involved in the
trade. At times, it was dangerous

Altes Spittel.

Gondo Gorge.

Kasper Stockalper by Georg Christoph Mannhaft.

because of brigands, armed invasions, border disputes and political unrest. It took a man of vision, Kaspar Jodak Stockalper (1609-1691), to see opportunities after the Thirty Years War in 1648 for commercial traffic. Up until then, the Simplon was a mule trail used mainly by smugglers. Stockalper provided a safe passage of goods and at the same time, gained control of the commerce through the Simplon and in the Valais. By 1650, he employed some 200 muleteers and had a small police force. The key to his success was to build numerous storehouses along the trail so he could market products at the most advantageous time. He also had the profitable monopoly of the salt trade and operated the postal system between Italy and the Netherlands. During Lent, he even controlled the import of snails into the Valais which were eaten by poor people who could not afford fish.

Stockalper was the richest man in the Valais and built the Baroque Castle of the Three Kings (Stockalper Castle), the Jesuit College and the convent of St Ursula in Brig. He also owned the gold mine in Gondo-Zwischbergen, the copper mine in Val d'Herens and the iron mine in Grund Ganter. He was showered with honours by kings and emperors, and nicknamed the 'King of the Simplon' by Louis XVI. But he overstepped the mark when he showed partiality to the Hapsburgs and was accused of treason. Most of his fortune was confiscated because of unpaid taxes and he was exiled to Domodossola, Italy. He returned to the Valais in 1685 where he died.

Napoleon, another visionary, built the road over the Simplon as part of his military strategy so that he would have a secure link between Italy and France. In September 1800, three months after the battle of Marengo, he ordered that the road from Brig to Domodossola be accessible to artillery. He had experienced his first crossing on the Stockalper trail on the back of a mule when he was with the Reserve Army on his way to a campaign in Italy. The low altitude of the Simplon and its relatively scanty snowfall determined his choice rather than Mount Cenis over the French Alps to Italy. The undertaking was entrusted to the engineer Nicolas Céard who drew up plans for a road 22-25 ft wide with a maximum gradient of 10%.

When the Simplon road was finished in 1805, it was one of the most modern in Europe and a masterpiece of engineering.

Stockalper Tower, Gondo.

Napoleon also built a hospice at the summit which could be used as a barracks. Gondo is the last village on the Swiss side of the border between Switzerland and Italy. A gorge leads into it and in a few places you feel hemmed in by the high granite cliff walls. The huge mass of rock is pierced by the Gallery of Gondo, a tunnel which you pass through on your way and it has a Napoleonic inscription 'Aere Italo 1805 Nap. Imp'. At the far end is the confluence of Alpienbach and the Diveria whose falls join at the foot of a spur. The Romans thought that the Gondo gorge could not be bridged and it was only in the 17th century that Stockalper built a bridge across it.

The Stockalper Tower dominates Gondo and has a commanding view across the border. It was built in 1670 as a coaching inn and is an example of Swiss Gothic style with its eight-storey tower and small windows usually found in fortresses or castles. It was here in this strange building in 1790 that the 20-year-old William Wordsworth spent a night. His visit to Gondo would have an enormous impact on his perception of the sublime in the future.

Another building of note in the village is the church of Saint Marc which dates back to the 15th century. There is a stone nearby which commemorates the victims of a mudslide that occurred in 2000. At the end of the 19th century, there was a revival of gold mining in the lateral valley of Zwischbergen. A French company which operated the mine extracted gold through the rock crushing method. By 1870, they employed 500 workers and

The Simplon Pass Eagle.

slabbed roofs has a distinct character from the other mountain villages with their wooden buildings. The Ecomuseum, housed in the Alter Gasthof (14th-18th century) is a real gem. This miniature museum has fascinating exhibits of everything you need to know about the Simplon pass from its people to its commence, including the first flight across the Alps in 1910 by Geo Chavez. The Perren collection, for example, ranges from products made from soapstone, spindles used in spinning wool, cream ladles to skim off the cream, pretzel irons with coats of arms and bands for hats that cost nearly as much as a pregnant cow. Opening hours – June 15-August 31 open daily from 13:00-17:00. The rest of the year: Wednesday to Sunday from 13·00-17:00. Closed November-March.

published a daily newspaper. Although the company had anticipated a yield of 10 gm of gold per ton, they only managed to achieve 3 to 4 gm and the company closed down in 1897. The Stockalper Tower has a small museum on the gold mine and there are still opportunities for visitors to prospect for gold.

Nowadays, the hiking trail, known as the 'via Stockalper', has been preserved over its entire length of more than 21 miles and has become a cultural and historical trail from Brig to Gondo. Look out for the remarkable 17th century Altes Spittel on the way. It can be rented for groups. Ideal for a sales conference. Tel.027 922 4642 or email: erich.bumann@vtg.admin.ch

The tiny Simplon Dorf (1490m) with its 17th-century stone houses and granite

The Sennerei is the cheesemonger who sells special cheeses from the Simplon. He has an Alpenrose cheese made with Alp roses and Alp cheese which is called Hobel cheese. There are also a good range of yogurts and pasteurised and unpasteurised milk. The Tea room bakery which is run by the fifth generation of the Arnold family has unique patisserie you can't find anywhere else in the Valais. There's Simplon Heart biscuits, Baconrind cakes (Speckschwarte) and the Rye bread which is made from leaven that dates back to a century ago. A striking feature of the pass is the stone sculpture of the Eagle by Erwin Baumann which was built by the Swiss army during the Second World War. It's the symbol of the mountain brigade and is over 9 m high. Baumann used an innovative sculpting technique to create the monumental work.

Geo Chavez, Ecomuseum.

Sightseeing in and around Gondo

Gondo Gorge

In the summer of 1790, the young William Wordsworth and his friend Robert Jones set out on a walk through France and Switzerland at the rate of about 30 miles a day. On the morning of August 17, 1790 they crossed the Simplon on the Stockalper trail. It had taken some five hours to reach the pass and even longer on the other side as they had got lost.
They met a peasant who showed them a shortcut through the Gondo gorge. The characteristics of the ravine, the Romantic poet said, "Were all like the workings of one mind, the features, of the same face."

In book VI of the Prelude which was written some 14 years later, Wordsworth described several parts of the walk in detail. His passage through the Gondo Gorge represents some of the most remarkable lines he ever wrote: "The immeasurable height. Of woods decaying, never to be decayed, The stationary blasts of waterfalls, And everywhere along the hollow rent, Winds thwarting winds, bewildered and forlorn, The torrents shooting from the clear blue sky.

Thirty years later, he undertook a second journey along the Simplon, this time with his sister Dorothy. In her journals she described Wordsworth in the Stockalper Tower. How he lay in the high and spacious room with its little grated windows in a state of "melancholy among weary bones.""

The Regions

Visp

Visp is the most important rail hub in the Valais, replacing Brig once the Lötschberg base tunnel was built. It stands at the head of the two valleys which lead to the renowned resorts of Zermatt and Saas-Fee. Zermatt has the Matterhorn – the most famous landmark in Switzerland. It was put on the world map in July 1865 when Edward Whymper led the first ascent of the peak in July 15, 1865 and four of his party of seven died in the descent when the rope snapped. Zermatt is a car-free resort and has a lot to offer on a day trip as it has good train connections. There are always crowds as there is no off-season and backpackers rub shoulder to shoulder with the rich.

Saas-Fee is in the next valley and is surrounded by 13 of 4,000m peaks. It has been named the 'pearl of the Alps' and situated at the foot of the glaciers. The resort which is one of four linked villages in the Saastal can only be reached by bus or car. The whole of the Saas valley is accessible by post bus that passes Eisten with its Neo-Gothic church, then Saas Balen, Saas Grund and Saas Almagell before reaching the Mattmark Dam. It's the largest earth dam in Europe and also a pilgrimage site.

CULTURE OF MASKS - TRADITION OF OUR LORD'S GRENADIERS

THERMAL BATHS - GEMMI PASS

THE BEST PRESERVED TRADITIONAL MOUNTAIN VILLAGE, ALBINEN

THE ALBINEN LADDERS

The Regions

Leuk

The Lötschen Valley

At a glance

Culture of Masks

The most unique feature of the valley is the masked Tschäggätta (pronounced chagatta). For a period of 3 weeks until Lent (February until March), people parade around in groups or individually. If you don't spot them then all is not lost for Kippel has a museum with an exhibition of masks as well as a film of them.

The Tradition of Our Lord's Grenadiers

The Valaisans were once mercenaries who fought in foreign wars. The soldiers who died are commemorated on the religious feast of Corpus Christi when the local men dress in ancient uniforms and take part in a procession.

Hiking and skiing

In summer there are 124 miles of hiking trails. In winter, a glacier ski area with numerous medium-difficulty pistes and a free-ride area as well as winter walking trails with panoramic views of the Alpine 4,000ers

Hotels

It's worthwhile using the valley as a touring base because it's unspoilt. There are 11 hotels and 182 apartments. The cosy Nest and Bieschhorn in Ried was a favourite of the English climbers in the 19th century, among them Sir Leslie Stephen. It fits snugly between the Bernese Alps and the Bieschhorn. The Edelweiss hotel is situated in Blatten, the last village of the valley. It is quiet and has a large sun terrace. The Fafleralp is off the beaten track and surrounded by majestic summits and panaoramic views.

Restaurant

Lonza in Wiler uses local produce and serves bio food. It has the special dessert of Chächlini, a bread cake and Belper Knolle cheese seasoning for pasta.

Tourist office

Lötschental Tourismus
CH - 3918 Wiler
Lötschental
Wallis (VS)
Tel. 027 938 88 88
www.loetschental.ch/en

Lötschen Valley.

Swearing in ceremony.

The Lötschen valley's geographical isolation led to the development of unique forms of culture. It's situated between the Bernese and Valaisian Alps and when you emerge from the Lötschberg tunnel into the hamlet of Goppenstein, you drive up and reach a stunningly beautiful valley through which the Lonza river meanders. The first village is Ferden, past the photogenic Kippel with its wooden houses and into the main community of Wiler which has the tourist office and the cable-car station up to the Laucheralp. There are five communities including Steg, and hamlets such as Faflereralp, Laucheralp and Ried are strung along a 6-mile valley floor. On both sides are Alpine ridges topping some 10,800 ft and at the head of the valley is the Long Glacier. It's the

Masks at Kippel museum.

tongue of the Aletsch Glacier and is part of the UNESCO World Heritage Jungfrau-Aletsch zone.

The distinctive feature in the mysterious Lötschen valley is the culture of masks called Tschäggätta. For generations, a story was told of how the tradition began. It's the tale of the 'Schurtendiebe aus dem Giätrich' or the 'Beggar thieves' from Giätrich – an area opposite Kippel on the northern side of the Lonza. According to the legend, strange people lived in Giätrich. During the night, they dressed in wild clothing and attacked the prosperous Wiler. Ruins were found of such a settlement which existed 1,000 years ago. There are two other versions and the most conventional is that the masks were used to chase away winter and evil spirits. The third is the 'Bullbell War', trinkelstierkrieg (1550) where men dressed up in special outfits and masks in protest against the Church's proposed ban against the Tschäggättä.

The Tschäggättä, who appear between February 2nd and Ash Wednesday, look fearsome in their costumes. Their faces are covered with gruesome masks, on their backs and chests are sheep or goatskins and they wear belts with cowbells. To reinforce their wild image, their feet are often covered in sacks which obliterate their prints in the snow. They also wear gloves which are sometimes dipped in soot to blacken their victims' faces. They go about alone or in groups frequently ringing cowbells or else they spring out suddenly from unexpected places. Once there was a strict rule which only allowed bachelors to dress as Tschäggättä but

Dorfkeller, Kippel.

nowadays it's a free-for-all as anyone can participate. The highlight is the annual carnival parade in Wiler on the Saturday before Ash Wednesday and the Tschäggättä parade on the Thursday before Ash Wednesday.

The other memorable event in the Lötschen valley takes place at the end of May, beginning of June during Fronleichnam or Corpus Christi. 'Red soldiers' or 'Our Lord's Grenadiers' parade through the streets. The soldiers are descendants of mercenaries who fought abroad. For example, in the Siege of Lerida, Catalonia (1644), when Spanish forces attacked the French in the town, six soldiers from Lötschental died. A white silk banner with a red cross emblazoned with the year 1625 and the symbol of the era is stored in the church archives in

Kippel. The uniform of white trousers and scarlet jackets with gold buttons originated from a time when the men were in the service of Versailles and Naples. Their colourful outfit is topped with a hat and tall feathers. A sword is hung from a white criss-crossed band with a bullet pocket.

In the summer there are over 124 miles of hiking trails. The walk from Laucheralp across the Lötschen Pass into Bernese Oberland to Kandersteg ranks among the classics of the region. Fafleralp at the end of the valley is the starting point of the high route across the south-facing Alpine pastures through to Laucheralp. One of the most popular trails is the glacier of Falferalp – of which there are three options. Another trail takes in the legend of a countess who lived in castle tower on the black lake. She was wealthy and had many suitors who all tried to climb up the tower but failed, only to fall into the waters below. One day a man arrived with his strong son who managed to climb up to the tower. But the countess startled him with her eyes and he fell into the lake and died. The man cursed the countess and shortly after a hurricane destroyed the castle. Thereafter, a white snake with a crown on its head can sometimes be seen in the lake. Some say it's the ghost of the countess.

The ski area is the south-facing, sunny Laucheralp above the village of Wiler, with attractive facilities for families. The cable car takes you up to the Märwig/Gandegg region and up onto the Hockenhorngrat (10,206 ft), a glacier ski area with numerous medium-difficulty pistes and a free-ride area. It also provides a winter walking trail at over 9,842 ft with

Preparation of meat for drying.

panoramic views of the Alpine 4,000ers or the mountain summits of over 13,123 ft. For cross-country skiers, there's a long trail on the valley floor, an illuminated night trail in Kippel and a demanding ascent trail onto the Laucheralp.

The villages are mostly made up of closely grouped houses built of intersecting larch trunks or 'blockbau' which rest on stone foundations. Kippel was first mentioned in 1213 and has the notable residence, the Great House (1665), now a restaurant called the Dorfkeller. The church is worth a visit if only to see the three-tier main altar, the polygon pulpit with the stone base and the statues of the Evangelist that date from 1694. The museum with its fascinating collection of masks is a must. It also has fine examples of traditional costumes, worn on festive and religious occasions. Each village and region in the Valais has their own distinctive style. An oddity in the museum is an old wooden cross which is used by the Prefect of the region to swear allegiance.

There are various Baroque chapels in the valley but the one at Kühmad which is between Blatten and Fafleralp is special. It's a site of pilgrimage and a Kraftort or sacred site of the Celts.

The Bieschhorn (12,906 ft) which shelters the valley from the south side was first climbed by Sir Leslie Stephen. During the 'golden age of mountaineering' the first hotel, Nest and Bieschhorn, was opened in Ried between Wiler and Blatten, in 1868. It still welcomes guests today.

Leukerbad

At a glance

Thermal baths

Nude bathing in the Roman-Irish baths at the Lindner Alpentherme, combining traditions of both cultures; the public Burgerbad with its 10 pools and natural rock grotto; Volksheilbad which offers physiotherapy; and the private baths at hotels like the Mercure Bristol.

Gemmi Pass

It's about a two hour hike up the pedestrian-only pass. Take a walk around Dauben lake and descend by foot or by cable car.

Hiking and skiing

In summer there are 124 miles of hiking and mountain biking on either the Torrentalp or Gemmi. In winter there are 31 miles of ski slopes for beginners or experienced skiers.

Breakfast in the thermal bath

Both the Burgerbad and Lindner Alpentherme offer breakfast in the bath.

Activities and events

One is spoilt for choice for the family from tennis, ice skating to paragliding, catamaran sailing, rock climbing and fishing. Events include carnival with Guggenmusik, cow fighting, a shepherd's festival, country music and a wine festival.

Leukerbad.

A thermal spa.

Tourist Office

In a modern building above the Rathaus
car park.
CH-3954.
Tel. 027 472 7171
www.leukerbad.ch

Leukerbad is the oldest and one of
the most celebrated thermal spas in
Switzerland. Over the centuries it has
attracted famous visitors from the
physician Paracelsus, Goethe, Guy du
Maupassant and Mark Twain to Picasso,
Paul Valery and James Baldwin. There
are 30 baths in this modern hot springs
complex which offers a range of saunas,
steam rooms and a variety of treatments
including massage. You also have a choice
of three separate wellness areas.

The Burgerbad is the largest with 10
pools and a natural rock grotto where
you can relax in warm thermal water. It
comes directly from the spring and has a
temperature of 43°C. The pools are also
equipped with huge waterslides. The
Lindner Alpentherme is more select with
both an indoor and outdoor pool as well
as the mixed gender Roman-Irish bath.
The combination of Irish and Roman
bathing traditions was invented by Dr
Richard Barter in the 19th century. The
treatment uses various thermal and hot-air
baths. The body is warmed, cooled and
purified in 11 stages. The Volksheilbad
spa uses thermal water directly from
the spring, has an aromatherapy steam
room and an infrared cabin. Health and
beauty treatments are also available.
Private thermal baths can also be found in

hotels like Les Sources des Alpes and the Mercure Bristol.

The wellness programme offered by Leukerbad extends beyond massages, saunas and hot springs, however. It comprises a comprehensive healthy lifestyle which includes fitness, nutrition, rest, sports and fresh mountain air. Specialised treatments are carried out by, among others, physiotherapists and acupuncturists. There is also a rehabilitation centre which takes care of patients with musculoskeletal and neurological disorders, post-operative problems and post-traumatic conditions in the locomotory system.

But Leukerbad is more than just a thermal spa. As it lies in a valley surrounded by mountain ranges it offers 31 miles of ski slopes up to 8,562 ft for beginners and experienced skiers. During the 'Golden Years of Mountaineering', Leukerbad was an essential stop-off for travellers. It was on the Thomas Cook tour and the journey marked the end of the renowned crossing of the Gemmi Pass which starts from Kandersteg in the Bernese Oberland and ends on the Valais slope in a dizzy road cut out of rock. Today, the same grandiose spectacle of the Bernese and Valaisian Alps from the natural pulpit of Gemmi can be easily reached via the cable car.

The Gemmi Pass was mentioned as early as 1252 and by 1677, there were regulations on the transport of people. "When a gentleman or lady wants to go to Leukerbad via the Gemmi and is heavier than average, he or she shall take 12 men; if they are of medium weight, 8 or 10 men; and if light, 4 or 6 men. As a reward

they shall be paid 20 batzen (10 centimes), half a measure of wine, bread worth half a batzen and half a pound of cheese." Some tourists found traversing the pass stressful and a guide, published in 1808, gave the following advice: "Once the terrible path is reached, the traveller faces backwards and is blindfolded before the bearers continue on their way singing."

Leukerbad was opened by Cardinal Schiner in 1501 as a thermal spring. It's an ideal base for touring as it's within easy reach of the Pfyn-Finges Nature Reserve, the vineyards of Varen and the historic town of Leuk. The Pfyn-Finges forest, an alluvial pine forest covering 1,000 hectares, is renowned throughout Europe for its rich variety of plants and wildlife. There are various guided tours around the forest and it's of particular interest to

Leuk

birdwatchers because of the wide range of rare species.

The village of Varen is the second largest wine producing area in the upper Valais. It is situated on the sunny slopes of the Bernese Alps and has stunning views of the Rhone and Pfyn-Finges forest. Leuk has been inhabited since the Roman era and is a pictureque village. There are also charming mountain hamlets nearby that are worth a visit such as Inden and Albinen.

But if you have little desire to explore, Leukerbad has a superb programme on site with over 1,000 events every year from concerts, carnivals, cow fighting, chess championships, curling to shepherd's and literary festivals and wine weeks. It's chock-full of activities from all-the-year round indoor sports of squash, tennis, badminton and table tennis to outdoor winter and summer sports. The official Swiss Snow Sports School is based in the village and besides the usual programme, there are many new additions like snow kites and Salto-trampolino. In summer, the spa outdoes itself with offers of fishing, rock climbing, catamaran sailing, golf, minigolf, tennis, Helsana Swiss running and walking trails, paragliding and even Monster scooters to make rapid descents from the Torrent cable car station.

Children are well catered for, too, and in winter there is a special Swiss Snow Kids Village with gentle slopes, slalom poles, tunnels, a magic carpet and a Pinocchio lift, among other things. In summer there are Punch and Judy shows, pizza-baking classes and candle-making workshops, or guided wild plant tours plus swimming.

The staff at Leukerbad take their slogan, 'energize your life' very seriously and visitors are guaranteed never to have a dull moment. They will certainly leave fitter than when they arrrived and with a sense of wellbeing.

Albinen.

Albinen.

Albinen

At a glance

Albinen

The village of Albinen is one of the sunniest in the Valais. Awarded the best preserved traditional mountain village.

The Albinen Ladders

The unique Albinen ladders can be climbed on a hike to Leukerbad. Not for those with a fear of heights.

God's Dwarf restaurant

The restaurant serves four-course menus with vegetables from their own garden.

The House of the Elves

A unique bed and breakfast experience – you can cook in the kitchen and they even offer a babysitting service.

Local pottery

Don't miss Albinen's pottery shop with artistic works.

Hiking and skiing

A free shuttle takes visitors to the cable car station at Flaschen for Torrentalp.

Tourist Office

Near the church.
CH-3955.
Tel. 027 473 4004
www.albinen.ch

The village of Albinen (4,183 ft) is situated on a steep slope above the Dala Gorge, on the sunny side of the Rhone valley. It is one of the most beautiful places in the Valais and a well-known example of a well-preserved traditional Swiss mountain village. Narrow stone

Dala Gorge by Caspar Wolf 1770.

The land owned by Albinen stretches from the Dala river (2,493 ft) to the Torrenthorn (9,832 ft) and encompasses little hamlets above or below such as Tschingere, Dorben, Tschaermilonga and Torrentalp. Local farmers lived a semi-nomadic life as the state of the pastures dictated their movement up or down the slopes.

In winter, the village is well placed for skiers and snowboarders with 31 miles of pistes around the Torrentalp. There is a free shuttle that takes visitors to the Flaschen cable station. The ski runs are suitable for beginners as well as advanced skiers. In summer, there's an extensive network of paths and biking trails. The paths run through meadows and larch forests and rise up to views of breathtaking beauty. The highlight is the route that takes in the Albinen ladders.

alleys run between old houses built out of tough larch timber. Many of the homes and storage buildings (raccard) are several hundred years old and demonstrate impressively the craft of former generations. The views of the valley, the Rhone and Pfyn-Finges forest below are spectacular.

The modern church is oval-shaped and stands at the centre of the village, dedicated to Saint Nicolas de Flue, the hermit. It's on the site of an earlier church that was built in 1739 after the village separated from Leuk. Inside is a Baroque altar and a 19th century organ made by Walpen of Reckingen. There are also examples of contemporary art. Alfred Grünwald created the stained glass windows and Elio Sello, the wood carvings of the Stations of the Cross.

Albinen is a hospitable village and every week offers an apéro or aperitif on Monday and a free guided tour on Friday. It is also full of surprises. There is the House of Elves B&B, a God's Dwarf restaurant and a pottery shop, Toepferhuus. A regular bus service is maintained to Leukerbad, Leuk and its railway station.

Albinen.

St Stéphane church.

Leuk

At a glance

Architecture

An architectural gem with examples of 13th-16th century buildings.

'Danse Macabre'

An extraordinary charnel house with a painting of the 'Danse Macabre'.

Oldest grapevine

See a grapevine dating from the 19th century and taste the Vitis Antiqua wine.

Pfyn-Finges park

Spectacular views of the wild Rhône from the massive alluvial cone and the Pfyn-Finges park.

Hiking and Golf

Hike through the Pfyn-Finges forest or explore Leukerberg mountains. A good map of trails can be found on the website. Relax with a round of golf on the 18-hole course.

Tourist Office

At Leuk station.
CH-3952. Susten.
Tel.. 027 473 1094
www.leuk.ch.

Leuk or Leuk-Stadt is on the Albinen-Leukerbad road. From whatever direction you drive along the Valais, two buildings in Leuk catch your eye – the Bishop's castle with its glass cupola and the Town Hall tower with its four turrets. The prominent position served a purpose because during the Roman era, it was a

Angels in Ringacker chapel.

Charnel house, St Stéphane church (below).

fortified town, a Leuca fortis, from which its name is derived. The inhabitants could see their enemies approach either from the east or the west. It was given the honourific title of 'city' or 'stadt' by the Bishop because at one stage, it was a thriving community with some 40 mills.

Leuk is a treasure trove of historic buildings, alleyways and cobbled streets packed in a small area which all serve to convey you back to the 15th and 16th century. You can see the manor houses of the ancient families of von Werra, Zen Ruffinen, Mageran and Albertini and the 13th century Town Hall and the Bishop's castle. The castle or "Scoundrel's Tower", first mentioned in a document in 1254, was the scene of torture, death, peace treaties, a regional parliament and, in the 17th century, witch trials. At present, the famous Swiss architect, Mario Botta, is involved in a restoration project which includes the construction of the glass cupola. Once completed, it will unite the past and the future. A multi-centre for education, art, tourism, leisure, meetings, information and communication. From the castle's esplanade at the entrance to the village is an astonishing view of the valley floor. From here you can see the great alluvial cone of rubble from the collapsed Illgraben mountain opposite.

The pièce de résistance of the historic architecture is the Gothic church of Saint Stéphane which was completed by the master builder Ulrich Ruffiner in 1514. Art pieces include the Meschler altar, the pulpit, paintings and statues. In 1982 a gruesome discovery was made in the crypt behind a wooden wall. It could have been a scene from a horror movie. When the wood was knocked through, the builders faced a spine-chilling 65 ft wall of skulls. It was a charnel house chapel of over 20,000 skulls, piled 10 ft high. Once the cemetery was full, the priests had used the crypt as an extension and as a store for ecclesiastical treasures. However, the room also held further surprises. There was a 'Danse Macabre' cycle of frescoes and a collection of 26 fine Romanesque sculptures that dated back to the 12th century church of which only the bell Tower remains today. And if the scene was not grisly enough, an inscription of the memento mori read: "That you are, we once were. What we are, you will become."

The other church, the Ringacker, built outside the village in 1694 on the old plague cemetery, is representative of Valaisian Baroque architecture. It has a monumental triaxial main altar (1705) by J. Sigristen, rich stucco on the walls, late Baroque statues as well as a Baroque organ by Matthäus Carlen who began a dynasty of organ builders. Of note is the monstrance and 200 angels. This rich architectural heritage escaped pillage of its artworks by the victorious Napoleonic troops that followed the battle with the Upper Valaisians in 1799 at Pfin-Finges.

Also on Leuk's doorstep is the largest stone pine forest in Central Europe which grew on the fluvial cone as minerals in mud provided the nutrients for tree growth. It has an unrivalled biodiversity with over 470 different types of plants and some 130 different species of birds. The forest is ideal for hiking and has countless signposted trails.

'Vitis Antiqua' vine.

But not to be outdone in the wine stakes, Leuk has the oldest red grapevine that dates back to 1798. Cuttings have been taken from the Cornalin 'Vitis Antiqua', propagated, replanted and a dark deep red and velvety wine has been made. There are several wineries in Susten which stock the wine including Kellerei Leukersonne which has award winning wines. Although small it's certainly worth a visit. The community has amalgamated with the village of Susten and they share Leuk station.

Illhorn canyon.

Sightseeing in and around Leuk

If you drive past the Illhorn (8,910 ft), opposite Leuk, you might not realise that its beige hue belies a serious state. Erosion had caused the mountain to collapse and form a canyon. The Illhorn, which is rather apt a name, has the most active debris flow torrents in the Swiss Alps with some 100,000 cubic metres a year.

The erosion slope measures an impressive six miles and consists of quartzite, limestone deposits and dolomite which is particularly susceptible to weathering. The canyon can be reached on foot in about an hour from Chandolin, providing you with stunning views down into the Rhone valley, or from Susten where you can see the reddish rock basin and the gigantic slide.

LONGEST FUNICULAR IN SWITZERLAND

MUSEUM OF WINE AND VINE - WINE ROUTE

LAKE OF GÉRONDE - VAL D'ANNIVIERS

The Regions

Sierre-Anniviers

At a glance

The Lake of Géronde

The lake has a sandy beach and great swimming facilities. La Grotte is a nearby hotel and restaurant.

The wine route from Sierre to Salgesch

This walk of about 2½ hours takes you from the top of Sierre, the wine museum to the other half of the museum in Salgesch.

The longest Funicular in Switzerland

The SMC station for the 2.6 mile trip is in the main avenue Général-Guisan. The last stop is Vermala in Montana.

Hiking and Skiing

In Grimentz-St. Jean, one of the six villages of the Val d'Anniviers, there's over 62 miles of walking trails. In the five resorts (Grimentz-St. Jean Zinal, St-Luc/ Chandolin and Vercorin), there are over 136 miles of ski slopes.

Val d'Anniviers

The side valley is one of the most picturesque in the Canton. There's an ice age landscape in the Vallon de Réchy and the spectacular Imperial Crown of three peaks.

Tourist Office

At the station.
CH-3960
Tel. 027 451 7116
www.sierre-anniviers.ch

Sierre

Sierre is one of the sunniest towns in Switzerland and for this reason its Latin name was Sirrum Amoenum, Sierre the pleasant. It lies in the valley below the vineyards of the Noble country and at the mouth of the lovely Val d'Anniviers. The town is a gastronomic centre of the Valais with top restaurants like the Terminus and the Château de Villa. The latter specialises in Valaisian dishes like air-dried meat, alpine cheese, rye bread and raclette and has a wine cellar, Oenotheque, that showcases some 600 Valaisian wines. The wine museum, Musée Valaisan de la Vigne et du Vin, is next door to the Château and gives an overview of the history and culture of wine in the Valais.

Wine was considered a food with the same nutritional value of soup – it jolted the body into life and kept one's strength up. The tradition was to offer a mother who had just given birth spiced, mulled Humagne Blanche and farmers in the mountain villages refreshed their thirst

Vinea wine festival.   Raclette cheese.

Author with bike from Valaisroule (below).   Valaisian plate of cheese and dried meat.

with wine in special wooden carved bottles.

It's worth exploring the wine route that links Sierre to Salgesch. You can either walk or take a free bike (issued at bike stations throughout the Valais). The route, some 4 four miles long, has an open-air museum where signs describe the different grape varieties such as Chasselas, Pinot,

down the wine route.

The 16th century Maison Zumofen, the wine museum, is in the quiet village of Salgesch, complementing the exhibition at the museum in Sierre. Several rooms cover the art of winemaking – the soil, grape varieties, techniques and tools, all conducted with the blessing of Saint Théodule, the patron saint of wine growers

The Wild Rhône.

Sylvaner and Malvoise, the quality of the soil and the various pruning methods. The longstanding tradition of vignolage, a contract between the owner of a vineyard and the grower, includes the provision of fife and drum music to accompany work in the springtime. When the grapes ripen during August and September, you can taste the different varieties. Wheel your bike from Valaisroule at Sierre station, onto the funicular up to Montana and ride

in the Valais.

The lake of Géronde, with its sandy beach, is south of Sierre. In an eastward direction lie half a dozen low rounded hills, the result of alluvial deposits and an ancient landslide. Behind Sierre, towards the south as you climb the road to Montana, you will discover the villages of Veyras, Miège and before Mollens the tower of Muzot where Rainer Maria Rilke lived.

Sierre-Anniviers

Matterhorn.

The jewels in the crown of Sierre are the picturesque villages which are strung along the Val d'Anniviers above the town. The name of the valley could be a synonym for seasonal because of the Anniviards nomadic lifestyle. During springtime, families descend on Sierre to work on the vineyards until mid-June when they ascend to the Alps to pasture their cattle and make cheese. Then in mid-September, they would return for the grape harvest before disappearing to their villages for the winter. Each community also brings along a school teacher and priest to officiate the Sunday service.

The area is a paradise for mountaineering as there are five 13,123 ft peaks (or 4,000ers as they are known by professional climbers) including the incomparable Weisshorn (14,780 ft) and Bishorn (13,123ft) – nicknamed the 'ladies' 4,000er' as it's relatively accessible. Another accessible 4,000er peak is the Breithorn, near the Matterhorn. The cable-car station is at 12,700 ft and is a good starting point.

Vallon d'Réchy.

Imperial Crown of Dent Blanche, Zinalrothorn, Weisshorn.

Val d'Anniviers is a cornucopia for downhill sports with 136 miles of pistes and 45 ski lifts in the four areas. The cluster of villages along the left side of the Valaisian Alps include Chandolin which is the highest village in the Valais, Vissoie, St-Luc and further up Zinal. On the right side, Grimentz and the Moiry Lake and Glacier.

Sightseeing in and around Sierre

The 13th century village of Chandolin is the highest in the Valais (6,351 ft) and in the 15th century belonged to Leuk. St-Luc is a delightful hamlet on the sunny side and well worth a visit as it offers an impressive panorama of mountain ranges specially the Weisshorn. It also reflects the past splendour of the Belle Epoque with the hotels of Bella Tola and Weisshorn (1883), perched on the edge of a mountain slope at 7,667 ft. St-Luc is also the site of the François-Xavier Bagnoud Observatory and has a planetary trail. An unforgettable sight on the way up to Zinal is the Imperial Crown – the peaks of Zinalrothorn, Weisshorn and Dent Blanche.

Grimentz is a pretty village known for the multitude of red geraniums that decorate the window sills and balconies and is

dotted with raccards – small barns on stilts for wheat storage. At its centre is the 16th century house of the Bourgeoisie which has the famous 'Glacier wine' in its cellar. The village is well worth a visit as is the Moiry dam and Glacier. When I first came to the Valais in summer and could not stand the heat in Sierre, I went up to Grimentz which was cool and picturesque.

Grimentz.

Grimentz.

Stilts under storage houses.

Ibex.

Chamois

The pièce de résistance of the Sierre-Anniviers region is the Vallon de Réchy which lies above Vercorin. The landscape has typical Ice Age features with glacial knobs, moraines and cirques -– steep-sided hollows formed by past glaciers. As you emerge from the cable-car station on Crête-du-Midi (7,650 ft) you are overawed by the view of the untamed, high valley with the Maya peak and Becs de Bosson (10,331 ft) in the distance. Yet, there's more as it's unspoilt with mountain lakes and streams – like La Rèche that meanders over boggy ground. The forests of pine, spruce, larch, stone pine and alder are places of refuge for a wide range of flora and fauna.

Marmot.

CASTLES ON THE TWO HILLS OF SION

GRANDE DIXENCE – THE TALLEST GRAVITY DAM IN THE WORLD

THE SAINT-LÉONARD UNDERGROUND LAKE

The Regions

Sion

At a glance

The castles on the two hills of Sion
Valère, with its fortified church, and
Tourbillon, and its ruined Bishop's palace.

Supersaxo Mansion
Supersaxo Mansion with its magnificent
sculpted ceiling is well worth a visit.

Zenhäusern or Z
The town of Zenhäusern or Z is the place
to see and to be seen. The pavement cafes
in rue du Midi are reminiscent of Paris.
The town has a superb patisserie and the
best coffee in town.

Grande Dixence
The tallest gravity dam in the world. There
are guided tours inside. It's also the start
of several hiking tours.

The Euseigne Pyramids
The Pyramids at the village of Euseigne.
You can't miss these stone jags – the road
to Arolla passes straight through them.

Wine and cheese
Wine tasting at Caveau-Oenothèque at
Grand-Point 29 or you may prefer the
chic wine boutique of Les Fils de Charles
Favre in Av. de Tourbillon. Grenette in
Grand-Point 24 is the place for cheese
but foodies will be knocked out by the
main Grenette fromagerie at Conthey
outside Sion with its range of 250 cheeses.
Raclette is good buy to take home.

Hiking and skiing
Hikes along the bisses of Clavau, Lentine
and Montorge. But the main area for
hiking and skiing is the Arolla valley.
Located at 2,000 m, there's a good chance
it will have snow longer than other resorts.
It's also en route for the trekking tours
like the Mont Blanc and the Chamonix –
Zermatt.
www.arolla.com

Tourist Office

Place de la Planta
1950 Sion
Tel. 027 327 7727
www.siontourisme.ch

Sion is the capital of the Valais and a town
full of secrets. Not many Valaisians know
that it is the oldest town in Switzerland.
And if you enter the Cantonal History
Museum, there is a further surprise as you
will find evidence of Neolithic habitation
through the anthropomorphous steles
and funerary items on display there. The
first farming community settled here
about 6,000 BC, first discovered from the

Adoration of the Magi by Master of Guillaume de Rarogne circa 1440.

excavations at la Planta square. It was once a well protected terrace created when the Sionne river (which is now enclosed under the rue Grand Point) flowed into the Rhone. The site between the two rivers was at the foot of two hills, the Valère and the Tourbillon, each crowned by fortresses. The town is also the oldest diocese in Switzerland with a Christian stone from 377 AD. This can be seen in the wall of the Renaissance Town Hall.

But Sion is much more than its long history. It's an exciting place because it has everything: an old town with pedestrianised cobbled streets and 16th century houses and inns (like 12 rue de Conthey); the rue du Midi which is lined with cafes like Paris; a Beaux-Arts Museum with incomparable Valaisian artists; the sumptuous 16th Supersaxo

Mansion with its famous ceiling; the Town Hall, an outstanding example of Renaissance architecture; international music festivals during the summer that include ancient organ music and a violin competition; the best shopping centre in the Valais; a sunny climate and charm of the Mediterranean; some 372 miles of hiking trails and skiing in the surroundings; and above all, the wines with the Grand Cru classes of Fendant,

Liturgical chest.

Hills of Tourbillon and Valere.

Ermitage, Dôle and Syrah.

From a distance, the two castles on lone hills seem to be the distinctive feature in the landscape. On the higher of the two, to the north, are the ruins of the bishop's castle of Tourbillon. Built in 1290-1308 and burnt down in the great fire of Sion in 1788 which devastated half the town. It was the bishop's summer residence and is reached via the cobbled rue du Châteaux to the left by the Town Hall. It has an extensive view down to Martigny and up to Leuk.

On the lower hill to the right, stands the old castle of Valère surrounded by towers and other ecclesiastical buildings. It's the largest fortified church in Switzerland and is dedicated to Notre Dame de la Valère (12th-13th century). With its interesting capitals, pictures and carved choir stalls, also of note is the wide, stone rood screen which separates the congregation and choir from the altar. The priest would stand on top of the screen to give his sermons. It has blind arcatures and the altar is lit by high windows, including a rose window. The wall paintings are the work of Peter Maggenberg and Etienne de Montbéliard in the 15th century, ordered by Bishop Guillaume V de Raron who had the privilege of being buried just inside the church, opposite the main door. You can see his chapel and tombstone in the nave. Another notable feature, high on the back wall just below the rose window, is the oldest playable organ in the world (1390) which is used in the annual festival of music.

In Sion itself stands the Gothic cathedral (12th-15th century) of Notre-Dame du Glarier and adjoining it, the elegant church of St Théodule which was built by Cardinal Schiner. It's on the site of an earlier church for pilgrims who came to see the relics of the saint and first bishop of the Valais, under the tall altar. Françoise Dubuis, an archeologist, discovered the ruins of a Roman bath as well as the corridors where the pilgrims once walked

and erstwhile friend Cardinal Schiner. When the bourgeoisie got rid of the Prince-Bishops, they built the Town Hall which featured the artistic ironwork of Luchs, the chancellery with its high table and woodcarvings by Zerkirchen and the admirable astrological clock on the tower.

There is also good selection of artists at the Cantonal Beaux-Arts Museum. In the collection are Raphael Ritz's Pilgrimage to Longeborne (1868) and Containing the Rhone (1888); Ernest Bieler's Mother and Child (1907); Edouard Vallet La Terre (1917); and Edmond Bille's Premier printemps (1907).

The Grand-Point, a street-cum-square, which was built over the Sionne river because of its incessant flooding, has some 20 patrician houses. It's in the heart of the

Dome of Notre Dame de la Valère.

Town Hall, Sion.

and the hole through which they saw the relics and dangled string to touch them.

The old mansion of the Supersaxo family in the Gundisgasse has a Renaissance ceiling painted and sculpted by the Italian Jacobinus Malacrida (1505), one of the most renowned works of wood of the Gothic period in the world. It was built by Georges Supersaxo to dazzle his rival

old town and a market is held there on Friday mornings. The square has a view towards the vine terraces. Other streets in the old town – the rue du Rhone, the rue de la Porte-Neuve and rue des Ramparts – all lead into the lively place du Midi.

Sion is the town of wine and the best place to start is at the Caveau-Oenothèque at Grand-Point 29. It stocks 150 wines

Grande Dixence Dam.

Longeborgne chapel.

and you can indulge in wine-tasting. Or you may prefer to visit the wine boutique of Les Fils de Charles Favre in Av. de Tourbillon. But the Sedunoise, which is named after the Celtic tribe, the Seduni, who settled here, goes a step further and offers the Walk of the Divine, La Balade des Divine. This is a tour around the town for the gourmand and takes about three and a half hours, during which you taste 10 wines and several dishes at various venues.

Sion is a good base for touring as it's well served by transport connections. Besides train connections, it has the largest bus station in Switzerland, serving 26 destinations. There is also a small international airport with charter and private flights.

Sightseeing in and around Sion

About two miles from Sion in the direction of the Val d'Herens is Bramois. There, up towards the mountain you will find the pilgrimage route into the Borgne gorges to the Longeborgne hermitage which nestles against the cliff. The chapel has a large collection of thanksgiving offerings, ex-votos, and is one of the most important in Switzerland.

The Saint-Léonard underground lake, which is situated between Sion and Sierre was formed by water infiltrating the gypsum bed and dissolving it little by little. The cave entrance is a gap in the mountainside and tours of the lake are carried out in large rowing boats. As you launch off into the water, you will find that the contrasting shades of colour give it an otherworldly atmosphere. It's cold, so it's best to take a jumper. But if you are in

need of sustenance after the visit there is a good restaurant next to the station called Buffet de la Gare.

In the other direction on the road to Martigny you'll find Chamoson and from there a road descends into Saint-Pierre-de-Clages which is the only 'Book village' in the Valais. It has a 12th-century church which is masterpiece of Romanesque

St Leonard underground lake.

art with an octagonal belfry inspired by St Marcel church in Cluny, France. But there's more to this little village – it has good wineries. Cave du Vidonne has red wine Baton Rouge which is forbidden in Italy. It's made from a combination of Barbera grapes which is used for cheap wine and Sangiovese grapes which produces the expensive Chianti. John and Mike Favre's wines can be sampled at a restaurant up the road in Chamoson called Chez Madame. La Pleine Lune has a wine bar where you can try their full range with raclette or steak tartare from the special Herens breed of cattle.

PIERRE GIANADDA FOUNDATION

ST BERNARD DOG MUSEUM - DINOSAUR FOOTPRINTS

ROMAN AMPHITHEATRE

The Regions

Martigny

At a glance

Pierre Gianadda Foundation

With its international art exhibitions, the vintage car museum, the permanent exhibition of Leonardo da Vinci inventions, the Gallo-Roman collection and the sculpture park which includes Henry Moore, the Foundation is a must.

Old town or Bourg.

Wander along the cobbled streets among 17th century buildings. The restaurant Chez Pierre has a good ambience and food.

St Bernard Dog Museum

The museum provides a comprehensive review of everything you need to know about the St Bernard. St Bernard dogs are kept on site.

Roman amphitheatre

The amphitheatre seats 5,000 and holds many events like cow fighting.

Boulangerie Michellod

The bouangerie has a good selection of cakes and is in the main avenue of de la Gare.

Morand distillery shop

To sniff and savour a Williamine, a star among the fruit brandies, is a tradition dating back to 1889. The shop has an outstanding collection of brandies, liqueurs and syrups, and the miniatures in tin boxes make excellent presents.

Hiking and Skiing

Besides walks along the watercourses, the main trail is the Via Francigena, which is the pilgrimage from Canterbury to Rome. There is a stretch from Martigny to the Abbey at St Maurice or in the other direction from Martigny to Aosta across the Grand St Bernard Pass. Skiing can be found in the valleys south of Martigny including the famous Verbier and there are 298 miles of ski pistes.

Thermal Baths

The baths are within the neighborhood of Saillon and Ovronnaz and a good place to relax after your activities.

Batiaz Castle

The 13th century castle sits on the hillside and has a tavern for the weary traveller.

Mont Blanc Express

If you are so near Europe's Highest mountain, it's tempting take the scenic train to Chamonix and experience a panoramic view of all the Alps. A trip of a lifetime.

Tourist Office

Avenue de la Gare 6
- CH-1920
Tel. 027 720 4949
www.martigny.com

The biggest attraction in the town is the Pierre Gianadda Foundation followed by the Roman ruins and the St Bernard Dog Museum. Martigny is also the home of the

Bourg.

famous Swiss pear brandy, Williamine. But nothing is as charming as the old town or Bourg with its 17th century buildings like the Three Crowns turreted house and the Town Hall with its arcades. On his visit to Switzerland in 1802, the English artist J.M.W. Turner made a watercolour of 19th century Martigny, highlighting the cabriolet in which he travelled and the inn, Le Cygne, which was popular with British visitors at the time.

Martigny is located on the Rhone elbow where it heads towards Lake Geneva and is the hub of the pass routes across the Simplon, Great St Bernard and Forclaz. It was the site of a famous battle of Octodurus (as the town was known then) when the 12th legion and cavalry under Servius Galba fought the Gauls. It was mentioned in Caesar's account of the Gallic wars and the Gallo-Roman ruins include the amphitheatre which was built during the 2nd century BC and seated 6,000; the Domus of domestic genius; and the Temenus and Mithraeum which is the only sanctuary dedicated to the sun god Mithras open to the public in Switzerland.

There are wild valleys along the pass routes that lead to the Grand-St-Bernard Pass. The first is the Val d'Entremonts, which starts with the village of Sembrancher with its street fountains rich in natural fluoride, then up to Orsières with it's Gothic bell tower. From there a zigzagging road above leads to the charming Champex-Lac with its 19th century hotel, glacial lake and the best Alpine garden in Switzerland – with over 3,000 plants. The second is the Val Ferret, entered through a branch road from Orsières and has spectacular scenery. It extends for some 12 miles between two towering peaks, Mont Dolent with its two glaciers and the Mont Blanc massif. Val Ferret is an acclaimed bird-watching area where you can find rare, red-billed choughs, yellowhammers and kestrels. At its head on a plateau at 8,038 ft lie three Fenêtre lakes.

The main road from Orsièrs continues to

climb up to the village of Bourg-St-Pierre which has a Roman milestone dating to 300 AD and then at 8,103 ft you arrive at the Grand-St-Bernard Pass with the famous hospice. It was the archdeacon of Aosta, Bernard of Menthon who built the hospice to provide free shelter and food to pilgrims. He was beatified shortly after his death in circa 1080. The pass is the oldest Alpine route and the only road between

Mont-Blanc Express.

northern and southern Europe. Hannibal and his elephants used it as well as Julius Caesar. By the 18th century, some 20,000 people were using the road annually. Napoleon, who led his army of 40,000 troops across the pass into Italy in May 1800, ran up a bill of 40,000 francs before his departure. Almost 22,000 bottles of wine, a ton and a half of cheese and 1,763 lbs of meat were consumed and the bill

was never totally settled.

Martigny is also the gateway to the region for walks and to four valleys with 298 miles of ski pistes. After hiking or skiing, there are two thermal baths in Saillon and Ovronnaz where you can relax. It's also close to Europe's highest mountain, Mont Blanc, which can be reached easily by road or by the 'Mont Blanc Express'. There are two interesting villages which are nearby, Fully which is often called the chestnut and Petit Arvine capital and Les Marecottes with its Alpine zoo. For wine lovers Fully is a must because the top Valais wine grower, Marie-Thérèse Chappaz is based there.

The Trient valley

The history of the Trient valley – another important gateway from Martigny to France – is associated with the Grand Tours undertaken by young, upper class Englishmen between university and the beginning of a career. Part of their education during the 18th century was to travel through Switzerland and see the highest mountain in Europe, the Mont Blanc. The European aristocracy followed suit and in 1799, Goethe brought Karl August, the Grand Duke of Saxe-Weimar-Eisenach on a tour of the Valais. What impressed the German poet most was the sight of the 'Pissevache' waterfall in Miéville at the bottom of the Trient valley, between Martigny and St Maurice. He and the Grand Duke had travelled down the 'carriage route' which was cut out of the rock. "Finally, we stood in front of the waterfall, which deserves its fame above all others," said Goethe. "We climbed about and sat by the waters with a deep longing, wishing to stay for hours,

Emosson Dam.

no, rather to spend days of our lives in this enchanting place." The Mont-Blanc Express which started its service from Martigny to Chamonix in 1906 runs along one of the most scenic routes in Switzerland. You can admire the Trient Glacier, the view of the Balme Pass and the Emosson dam from the summits. Its route includes the villages of Salvan, Les Marécottes, Finhaut and Le Châtelard.

Finhaut

At a glance

Dinosaur footprints

Above the old Emosson dam, there are over 800 dinosaur footprints. A shuttle bus stops at the Emosson restaurant.

Emosson Dam

The dam lies at 2,000 m and can be visited from June 28th-August 29th. Free guided tours are offered daily at 11.30 and 3 pm except on Monday and Tuesday. It's the starting point for many walks and offers panoramic views of Month Blanc.

Tourist Office

It's in the station building.
Tel. 027 768 1278
www.finhaut.ch

Dinosaur footprints.

Finhaut (4,058 ft) is charmingly perched above the deep gorge of the Trient and has a fine view of the valley and the Trient Glacier. Once it rivaled Zermatt as the top Alpine resort with 17 splendid hotels, including the Hotel Giétroz and its vista of Mont Blanc, and its English church with its summer services – still open today. Originally, Finhaut (derived from Effeniaz, Finio, Fins-Tops and Figneaux) consisted of two villages, La Cotze and Le Léamon with a forest between them. During the Belle Époque and the period between the wars, it was a mecca for English tourists who among other things enjoyed the bottled radioactive water!

Many of the old buildings are still there including the elegant Bristol hotel near the station and the hotel Beau Séjour and pensions Le Mont-Fleury and Les Alpes. The Notre-Dame-de-l'Assomption, Our Lady of Assumption church, which was rebuilt in 1929 by the architect Fernand Dumas, is a masterpiece of sacred art in the Valais. The bright mustard coloured interior with open-beamed ceiling is the appropriate setting for the works of art. There is Alexandre Cingria's stained glass windows and triptych, the woodcarving of Francis Beaud, the embroidery of Marguerite Naville, the side windows of Eugene Marco Dunand and the painting of Marcel Poncet.

Finhaut is now an important base for trips to the Emosson dam, the Dinosaur tracks and the steepest cable car in the world. One of the most inspiring views of a dam can be found within a short distance from Finhaut. As you near the col de la Gueulaz, a narrow road rather than a pass, you have the feeling that you are on the top surrounded by peaks. When you arrive at the promontory with the Restaurant du Barrage d'Emosson you see the vista of the Emosson dam below – the second largest dam in Switzerland, built between 1969 and 1973.

Finhaut is the start of many hikes. The most interesting is up to the dam and to the site of fossilized Dinosaur tracks in the valley. It was an exciting discovery made by a geologist in 1976 from the Natural History Museum in Geneva, G. Bronner. There are over 800 footprints from nine species. The size of the footprints vary from 4 to 8 inches with a depth of 2.5 inches. The dinosaurs date from about 250 million years were mainly herbivorous. The average length of these animals was 10 to 13 ft and weighed 660 lbs to 880 lbs. Among those dinosaurs included in the discovery were the giraffe-like Prototrisauropus (23 ft tall) and the gigantic lizard shaped Pachysaurichnium (between 10 to 13 ft long). The dinosaurs lived near a beach until a movement of the plate tectonics broke the Earth's surface and forced a new mountain range skywards. They fell to their death and only their footprints remained. There are even fossilized ripples of sea sand. The real Jurassic Park is popular with visitors and can be seen in a gully on a high plateau above the old Emosson dam.

The hike to Châtelard theme Park takes you through Giétroz which has the oldest houses in the Trient valley dating from 1672. Both the hamlet and Finhaut were administered by the abbot of St Maurice who in the 13th century gave permission for communities of men to settle at Effeniaz. At one time, the only way to

reach Châtelard was to use a system of
ladders over the rocky terrain but in 1867,
it was replaced by winding paths. The
theme park offers three unusual rides in
mountain railways to the Emosson dam.
The first leg is on the historic funicular
with its gradient of 87%. The second
leg is in the Decauville panoramic train
with a 24 inches gauge which provides
superb views of the Mont-Blanc massif
and the Bouqui gorges. The final leg is by
Minifunic, a type of lift-cabin which rises
vertically and takes you to some 100 ft
above the dam. There you can walk along
the dam wall or along the lakeside.

Another route is to Tête Noir where a
circular trail leads to the mysterious
gorges. The trail crosses meadows, a
collection of piles of stones which have
to be surmounted by four ladders of larch,
followed by stone steps, over stonewalls
and terraces before it winds through the
forest to a bridge. There a path leads you
down to the gorge which towers high
above the river and affords a marvellous
view of the Cave of the Nymphs. At the
exit to the gorges of Tête Noir, the path
heads for Châtelard and the museum of
the CFF power station.

Besides hiking, Finhaut also offers
mountaineering, bungy jumping, mountain
biking and canyoning. After such
exertions, you can relax in the indoor
swimming pool which has a temperature
of 29°C and later, enjoy its sunny terrace.

THE WARMEST THERMAL WATERS IN SWITZERLAND

THE OLDEST CONTINUOUSLY INHABITED MONASTERY

MINIATURE STEAM RAILWAY - MONT BLANC

AQUAPARC

The Regions

Chablais

The region lies between the eastern shores of Lake Geneva and the peaks of the Dents du Midi. The Portes du Soleil spans the Swiss-French border with the mountain resorts of Champéry, Val d'Illiez/Les Crosets/Champoussin, Morgins and Torgon in conjunction with the French resorts across the border. It's one of the largest ski areas in the world with 403 miles of marked ski runs. In summer, some 24 chair lifts feed a network of biking, hiking and horse trails around 12 villages. The capital is Monthey.

At a Glance

Hiking and Skiing

In summer, hiking from any of the 12 villages with plenty of criss-crossing shortcuts. The Tower of Don (1998 m) is a little known mountain above Torgon and is one of the most beautiful trails in the region. You can reach the top, either on foot or by the Tronchey chair lift and you're rewarded by a scenic view of both Mont Blanc and Lake Geneva as well as Dents-du-Midi and the Combins. From the top, you can continue to the Col de croix and to the Savoyard side of the Portes du Soleil where you may catch sight of the shy mountain sheep. In winter, you have the largest ski areas in the world with 403 miles of marked ski runs.

Riding

Explore the French-Swiss Alps on horseback and stay a night in a gîte. There are equestrian centres in Champéry, Champoussin, Morgins and Les Crosets. The season lasts from June to October.

Treking Tours

There's the well-known Tour Dents du Midi mountains, a circuit of 42 km that takes about three days. Another is the Port du Soleil. It will take 33 hours to walk the French part and 15 hours for the Swiss one. In all, about a week of walking with some six to eight hours a day.

Thermal Baths

There are two thermal baths in the region. Lavey les Bains has the warmest thermal waters in Switzerland and is on the opposite bank of the Rhône from St Maurice or 10 minutes by train from Martigny and in the Canton of Vaud. The Thermal park in the Val d'Illiez has a swimming pool at a comfortable temperature of 32°C. and a river winding through the gardens with a waterfall and a grotto.

Lake Tanay.

Tourist Office

Place de Tubingen
CH 1870
Tel. 024 471 12 12
www.chablais.info

Champéry

Champéry in the Val d'Illiez is one of the oldest tourist destinations in Switzerland as the first hotel opened in 1857. It typifies the ski resorts found in the Portes du Soleil with easy access to the sunny ski slopes and the cable car that whisks the visitors up to 6,561 ft within 5 minutes. During the summer, there is horse riding, a via ferrata, canyoning, paragliding, bike competitions and musical events. The village has a fine view of the Dents du Midi with its steep off-white rocky face. It's there that the Défago galleries have been built, following a deep natural ledge across the cliff and providing a pleasant walk for tourists that is cool in summer. The Saint-Théodule church has a belfry fashioned in the shape of the Duke of Savoy's crown because he made a favourable impression on the villagers during a visit. On the lake shore, you find Bouveret and St Gingolph with sailing, water sports or cruising while further down in the valley is the historical site of the abbey of Saint-Maurice. There is also a thermal bath in Val d'Illiez.

Saint Maurice

At a glance

Abbey of St Maurice
It was built in 515 and is the oldest continuously inhabited monastery in the world. The church which existed in the 4th century was rebuilt several times. Of

particular interest are the stained glass windows which were created by Edmond Bille and illustrate the history of the martyrs.

Treasure Room

Pilgrims who have come to the abbey church for over 1500 years have left gifts. Some of the exquisite pieces include a Roman sardonyx vase, a golden jug from Charlemagne and sculpted head reliquary of St Candide.
Open: January, February, March, April / November, December 14:45*; May, June / September, October 14:45; July, August 10:30, 14:00, 15:15; Sundays and feasts: morning closed Mondays. *closed on Tuesday, Wednesday, Thursday, Friday unless a tour is arranged two days earlier by telephone.
Tel. 024 486 0404

Tourist Office

Saint-Maurice Tourisme Avenue des Terreaux
CH-1890 Saint-Maurice
Tel. 024 485 40 40
www.saint-maurice.ch

Saint Maurice was founded in the memory of the Roman soldiers of the Theban legion from Egypt who were massacred

Casket of Teuderic.

in 300 AD. They were Christians and refused to worship the Roman Emperor Maximilian. Their leader Maurice was canonised and in 380 AD, a sanctuary was built by the first bishop of the Valais, St Théodule, on the site of the necropolis of the former Roman city of Acaunum. The relics of the saint and his companions were first displayed there. In 515 AD, Sigismond, King of Burgundy built the

Reliquary of St Candide.

Abbey of Saint Maurice and since then it has been the oldest continuously inhabited monastery in the world. In the entrance hall of the monastery are remains of marble altars of the three gods worshipped in Acaunum: Mercury, Nymphs and Deo Sedato.

The church of the Abbey of Saint Maurice is hard up against the cliff and on the site

Sardonyx vase.

of earlier churches and includes elements from 11th, 17th and 20th centuries. The Romanesque tower which was integrated into the architecture in 17th century, has as the base of its arch, two Roman stones, one of which still has an inscription: "Dedicated to the gods that have taken the souls of Lucius Tincius Verecundus who occupied all the municipal offices." There is the tomb of Saint Maurice with an arcosolium and chapel. But the pièce de résistance is the series of stained glass windows in the five chapels by Edmond Bille, who took old texts about the saint and his legion to create the windows.

The other outstanding feature of the Abbey is the Treasure Room. Over the centuries pilgrims came to visit Saint Maurice which was on the via Francigena that connected Canterbury to Rome

and many brought gifts. There are fine examples of religious goldsmiths from Roman, Merovingian, Carolingian, Gothic, Baroque and Modern periods. Of note is the sardonyx vase (200-100 BC), the Teuderic casket (7th century), a large jug which reputedly belonged to Emperor Charlemagne (8th century), the casket of the sons of St Sigismond (12th century) and a masterpiece, the head reliquary of St Candidus (12th century) who was one of leaders of the Theban legion. Many of the items in the Treasure Room are still used in the liturgy and are part of the religious and cultural life of the Valais.

Sightseeing in and around Chablais

A pass for the birds

Above Champéry, which is west of Saint Maurice and in the Chablais region, is the bird pass between Switzerland and France. The low altitude of the Col de Bretolet (6,309 ft) makes it an ideal migration route and the pass has been turned into a nature reserve for the protection and study of the birds. The Swiss Sempach Bird Observatory operates a ringing station in the reserve which is popular with bird watchers. The migratory period is from early August to late October with many birds travelling during the night. One birdwatcher, Carlos Kruytbosch, who came with a party in the middle of September, observed some 27 species. Hundreds of house martens mixed with barn swallows swarmed around them for most of the day. Patches of shrub twittered with coal tits and every few minutes raptors passed over either alone or in pairs. Some 100 were seen in the four hours the party was there. The highlight was the sparrowhawk and the bearded or lamb vulture which spent most of the day lazily gliding around the valley or in and out of ravines. Then it was spotted gobbling a morsel on the ground, flopping about awkwardly on a scree. Later, it flew low and the birdwatchers had a close-up of the mask-like face and red eyes, that conveyed a monstrous and menacing appearance.

The observatory was established in 1958 and is manned 24 hours a day from June through to October. It has a comprehensive monitoring programme from documenting jays, tits and finches to studies of energy metabolism. The birds are caught in the retractable high or low mist nets. Once they are caught, their length and weight are measured and the age estimated from an examination of the back of their skulls. Coal tits, for example, weigh only a third of an ounce and a robin just over half an ounce.

Bouveret

At a glance

Beach
You can swim in the clean lake or play volleyball on the sandy beach.

Miniature Steam railway
Take a ride on the miniature trains at Swiss Vapeur.

Aquaparc
Bouveret's aqua parc has year-round entertainment for all the family.

Water sports
The town is a haven for water sports like windsurfing, water-skiing, kayaking or catamaran sailing and motor boats.

Cruises on Lake Geneva
CGN company offers cruises to places like Château Chillon, Lausanne, Vevey and Montreux in historic paddle steamers. There are piers at Bouveret and Saint-Gingolph.
www.cgn.ch

Hiking
There are trails for hikers and bikers on the Grammont mountain and the vallon of Tanay with its blue-green lake.

B&B
This is a stay with a difference as the B&B means Boat & Breakfast here.
Tel 079 301 9893
www.ladamedulac.ch

Learn to sail
The sailing school is Lac et Mer
Tel. 024 481 8361 or 079 622 0762

Ritz culinary course
A course or career in culinary arts can be taken at César Ritz Colleges Switzerland.
Tel. 024 482 8282

Grangettes Nature Reserve
A place to visit if you want to see a range of water birds. It lies on the opposite bank of the Rhône to Bouveret.

Tourist Office
At the railway station.
Tel. 024 481 5121
www.bouveret.ch

Bouveret is on the shore of the sparkling waters of Lake Geneva where the Rhone enters the lake. Once there were three outlets in the delta but in 1880 they were reduced to one channel through dam

Défago Galleries.

construction and correction work. The town lies in a bay between the Grangettes nature reserve and Saint-Gingolph, which was once a thriving boatbuilding centre.

The Grangettes nature reserve stretches from Bouveret along the shore of Lake Geneva to Villeneuve in Vaud and is a sanctuary for many migratory and waterbirds. Some 265 species have been recorded in the reserve which consists of humid forest, marsh and rushes. A variety of birds like ducks, gulls and cormorants winter here and the flooded reed beds provide an ideal habitant for the great crested grebes. A highlight of any visit is to see the mating behaviour of these striking, streamlined waterbirds. Their long slender necks are topped by a reddish brown crest and ear ruffs in the breeding season. Some 70-100 swim round frantically off the reedy shore, first separating into groups and then pairs. The pairs 'dance' around each other, raising and lowering their necks, flapping their wings, waggling their long sharp beaks and emitting high-pitched wailing and whinnying sounds. Then pairs may disappear into the reeds or return to the swarming group. The grebes have a characteristic to swim around with young on their backs. (Sir Julian Huxley did

a study on these waterbirds.) The best observation point is found at the mouth of the canal and at Les Saviez which is near Villeneuve. But there are also flora and fauna to be seen. There are rare groupings of yellow iris, bulrush and poison-hemlock and very rare species blossoming in the swamp like the lesser cat-tail, braun sedge, marsh peavine and sword-flag.

Bouveret is like no other resort of its size on lake Geneva with its two main attractions of the miniature railway and the water park. Who can resist a ride on a miniature steam train at Swiss Vapeur Park, where models resemble the locomotives of the British LNER or LMS and the American Union Pacific or New York Central. What's amazing, too, are the distinctive engines from the red Decauville loco with its black conical funnel to the twin engine Bayer of South African railways and the 141 R of the Montreal locomotive works. The park has a network which is built on two levels, with trains that run on 5 and 7¼ inch gauges through five tunnels and over ten bridges. All the buildings are exact replicas to scale. There's the famous George Washington Bridge, a church, a bank and the fortified medieval Aigle castle (1476) which is built to scale of 12.5 cm to a metre. The castle is even constructed with similar building materials to the original. There are pedestrian paths, picnic places and a cafe which was inspired by a Swiss farmhouse and also built to scale. If you can't wait long enough to hear the whistle of a steam train in Bouveret, just click on the website. (See the website. www.swissvapeur.ch)

The Aquaparc caters for families and

teenagers and is open all year round except for a short period of maintenance work. Like most water parks, it's filled with a variety of amusements including eight main water slides, splash pads, wave pool, bathing, swimming and is a barefoot environment. There are slides like the Booster loop that's operated by a trapdoor to a vertical descent into a steep loop. Excitement builds as you never know when the lifeguard will release the trapdoor. Another slide drops 82 ft in one shot. The parc also has a wellness centre, a gym, saunas, a hammam, and an indoor and outdoor pool. But it's unique because there's also access to the sandy beach on the lakeshore where you can swim in the lake. (It has an equivalent of a blue flag for cleanliness.) In winter, there are enough activities for five or six hours – even when it's snowing, you can sunbathe inside around the swimming pool area. There are two restaurants and a shop, which stocks a comprehensive range of swimwear in case you've arrived without a swimming costume or towel. Safety is paramount and lifeguards are on duty throughout the building.

The visits are streamlined through the introduction of an electronic wallet. This dispenses with the need to carry cash or worry about money. When you enter, you put a sum on deposit and in exchange, you are given an electonic watch. This opens your locker, pays your restaurant bill and when you leave, it informs you how much you have left. In fact, it doesn't allow you to exit unless you are paid back the remainder of your money.

The resort is good base to visit other towns along Lake Geneva. Historic paddle steamers cruise to places like Château Chillon, Lausanne, Vevey and Montreux. Also to France at Evian-les-Bains and Thonon-les-Bains.

Bouveret has hiking and bike trails. The Grammont mountain (7,125 ft) can be reached from the Tanay pass and provides views over Lake Geneva. Another hike is to the Vallon of Tanay and its blue-green lake which is encircled by rocky massifs. It has a microclimate with luxuriant vegetation and a wealth of wild life. But, the name tanay in the local patois is derived from lair or refuge for animals. Archaeologists have discovered caves that sheltered a prehistoric species known as cave bears which disappeared over 20,000 years ago. They also found flint and quartzite chips in a small shelter at an elevation of 5,905 ft, which belonged to Neanderthal man over 40,0000 years ago.

Bouveret is also home to educational institutions. There is the famous César Ritz Colleges Switzerland and the School of Missions, Tiberias. César Ritz, which was founded in 1982, was the first institution to combine the Swiss hotel hospitality tradition with the American science of management. It was approved by Mrs Monique Ritz of the César Ritz Foundation and now has two campuses, the Bouveret which is the Culinary Arts Academy, and the academic in Brig.

On the opposite side of Bouveret, you find Saint-Gingolph which for 500 years was at the centre of the cargo traffic on lake Geneva. It built the majority of barques destined to carry merchandise around the lake. At first, these sailing boats transported luxury goods and then mostly

Blair's Hut on the Montenvers by J.M.W. Turner.

heavy building materials like stone or wood. Its museum is worth a visit as it has exhibits including 33 model boats from the small, squat naus to the lateen-rigged barques, original vessels that only plied on Lake Geneva. There is also an interesting half-hour film which illustrates the history of the mercantile navigation of the lake. Saint-Gingolph is a border town with one half in Switzerland and the other in France. The Swiss inhabitants tend to shop on the French side because food like meat tends to be cheaper and they can find real croissant at the boulangerie. But although they live as Swiss citizens, when they die they become French because the only cemetery in Saint-Gingolph is in France.

Tiberias is a place of retreat and welcomes individuals, families and groups. It has a splendid modern chapel which overlooks Lake Geneva. For those who love sailing there's a sailing school too and if you want to live on board while you learn the ropes, a boat and breakfast.

Mont Blanc

"I profess myself to be a loyal adherent of the ancient Monarch of the Mountains, and ... no Alpine summit is, as a whole, comparable in sublimity and beauty to Mont Blanc." Sir Leslie Stephen., President of the Alpine Club from 1865–1868. He made first ascents of no less than nine peaks within 13 years.

On his visit to Switzerland in 1802, the cruel unpredictable ways of nature revealed in the jagged forms of the glaciers, scattered rocks or twisted trees, made elicited an instinctive response from J.M.W. Turner. The wild heart of the Alps, even the Sublime proved inadequate. And on the Mer de Glace with the view of Mont Blanc, he reached inside and became the first modern artist.

The climax to any visit to the Valais is to see the view from Mont Blanc, the highest mountain in the Alps. When you are on the summit, you look down on the rest of Europe. There is nothing to look up to as everything is below. It's the most spectacular sight. Grouped around you at unequal distances, as you stand on the platform of Aiguille du Midi, are innumerable white patches. One spot, for example, resembles the clustered peaks of the Bernese Oberland. A block as big as a pebble resembles the soaring Jungfrau, the terrible mother of avalanches. The snowy wastes of the Blümlisalp seem suspended above Bern, some 30 miles away. The little whitish brook represents the greatest ice-stream of the Alps, the huge Aletsch Glacier. For those who have plodded laboriously over it or along it, all have been impressed by the monstrous proportions. There below are the origins of the great rivers of Europe. One patch contains the main source from which the Rhine descends to North Sea. Two or three more sources overlook the Italian plains and encircle the basin of the Po and in a more distant group flows the Danube and below your feet the snows melt to supply the Rhone. Over there, is the Matterhorn, its angular dimensions are of infinitesimal minuteness. But within the small space one can recognise the precise configuration of the rocky ridges which the earlier climbers forced their way up from the Italian side. And if you glance below the platform, you might see a couple of climbers plodding upwards on

a narrow ledge, knee-deep in snow and you are bound to think what fools, what madmen. Just one slip would have been fatal to both. Nothing, moreover, is easier than to make one.

To experience the panorama from Mont Blanc, you take the Mont Blanc Express from Martigny to Chamonix. The railway is a narrow gauge and the electrification is provided by a third rail. The network stretches over 14 miles and passes through shady forests and breathtaking heights with views of waterfalls and rugged cliffs. The first stop in France is Vallorcine in the broad valley where you change trains. The line ascends again and the view of the Mont Blanc massif suddenly opens. In a matter of 90 mins you are in Chamomix and after a short walk you reach the cable car. Then up to the top station, Aiguille du Midi (12,604 ft) where you have a 360° view. Some 20,000 people climb the mountain every year.

Once in Chamonix you have an opportunity to travel on the Montenvers rack and pinion mountain train to see the glacier, Mer de Glace at 6,276 ft.

There was an amusing incident when Edward Whymper climbed Mont Blanc in 1864. He, the guide, Christian Almer and a companion had camped together on the Couvercle (7800) under a great rock. At 3.15 the next morning they started and left the porter in charge of the tent and food. They reached the summit at 10.15 am and there was a change in the weather. Snow began to fall heavily before they were off the summit rocks and their tracks were obscured and frequently lost. Everything became sloppy and so slippery that the

Tower at the Aiguille du Midi cable station.

descent took as long as ascent. They raced down to the Couvercle as they intended to celebrate their success and as they rounded their rock, a great howl broke simultaneously from all three. The porter had taken down the tent and was at that moment moving off with it.

"Stop there!" Whymper shouted. "What are you doing?"

The porter had thought that they had been killed or at least lost and was returning to Chamonix with the news.

"Unfasten the tent and get out the food," Whymper said. Instead, the porter fumbled in his pockets.

"Get out the food," they all roared as they had lost patience.

"Here, it is," the porter said producing a

dirty piece of bread covered with fluff. It was past a joke. He had devoured everything: mutton, loaves, cheese, eggs, sausages and wine. All was gone. It was idle to grumble and they decided to leave immediately. They were light and could move quickly. The porter was laden inside and out. He shuffled and trotted behind. He streamed with perspiration and the mutton and cheese oozed out of him in big drops. He larded the glacier. They had their revenge. They entered Chamonix at 8.15 pm amidst firing of cannon.

HOTEL OFENHORN
BINN   since 1883

Travel back in time and discover the rich traditions of Hotel Ofenhorn in the romantic and pristine Binn valley. You can still feel the spirit of the Belle Époque, the pioneer age of stately hotels, in our rooms, corridors and majestic dining hall. The creaking floors whisper many a forgotten secret.

The "Pro Binntal" cooperative was able to save and carefully restore this valuable building. Our rooms suit different accommodation standards and our kitchen offers local specialties and a wide range of delicious wines.

The Hotel Ofenhorn is the ideal starting point from which to discover the lovely Binn Valley, a nature park with dozens of gems. The valley has been protected since 1964 because of its scenic landscape, unspoilt villages, rich flora and, last but not least, its extraordinary abundance of minerals.

Come to Binn, to the valley of the hidden treasures.

www.ofenhorn.ch

Chapter 3

Fact File

The best sources of information are the Tourist offices. There are 110 offices in the Valais and they can provide visitors with lists from mountain guides, ski instructors to wineries and emergency services. www.valaisguide. co.uk has additional information on current events and complete lists of wineries, hotels etc.

Accommodation

The Valais is known for its two star and three star hotels which are usually family-run establishments and provide good hospitality and service. In some cases, the unusual accommodation is highlighted. More information can be found at:

www.swisshotelportal.ch
www.myswitzerland.com/de/hotels/index.
cfm/wallis
http://www.vs-hotel.ch

Albinen

Hotel Rhodania
Tel. 027 473 15 89
www.hotelrhodania.ch
The hotel is in quiet surroundings with 11 comfortable and cosy rooms. Free internet access via wirelss LAN. There is a beautiful view from its sun terrace.

La Demeure des Elfes
Tel. 027 473 16 54
www.lademeuredeselfes.com
This boutique bed and breakfast is located only 5 km from the ski slopes and a ten-minute drive from Leukerbad. Run by a Belgian woman, Véronique and her daughter Thessalia, they try to live up to the fairy-tale name by providing a magical atmosphere. The rooms combine modern furniture with traditional décor. All are ensuite and have a balcony or terrace with a view of the mountains. There are 9 bedrooms in total including family rooms. Breakfast is local breads, several kinds of home-made jams and mountain cheese. There is a baby-sitting service and pets are welcome. You can also relax in the garden and on the panoramic terrace. A large kitchen is also at the disposal of the guests, allowing them to prepare their own meals. Once or twice a week, the 'Elves' will invite guests to their table where their fairy fingers will have prepared dinner.

Arolla

Grand Hotel Kurhaus

CH-1986 Arolla

Tel. 027 283 70 00

www.hotel-kurhaus.arolla.com

The hotel lies in a pine forest at 6,889 ft and guests can ski just outside the front door as it's on the ski runs. In summer, there are many walks through the forest and paths to the alpine huts. It also has a special trail for nature lovers highlighted with information on the flora and fauna in the area. The hotel has a large terrace and spectacular views of the surrounding summits. "You've a wonderful feeling that you're in the Alps," said Peter Weatherill, the fourth generation of the family who runs the hotel and owns half the Arolla valley up to the Pigne d'Arolla. His great grandmother built the hotel in 1896 when English tourists were arriving at Sion station to spend holidays in the Alps. "They wanted to climb everything," he said. It took four years to build and the cement was made on the spot by burning limestone with clay. The first guest was the vicar H. Percy Grubb from London who blessed the establishment and it has been a success ever since. A member of the Swiss Historic Hotels, Ayurveda massage is available and there's free WiFi access.

Belalp

Hotel Belalp

Aletschbord 20

CH-2914 Belalp

Tel. 027 924 2422

website.www.hotel-belalp.ch

The Hotel Belalp was built in 1858 and

is perched on a ledge just above the Aletsch Glacier, with views of the old Aletsch Forests and the highest Valais peaks. It's ideally situated for hiking, glacier tours and winter sports.

Binn

Jägerheim

Ausserbinn
Tel. 027 971 11 31
www.jaegerheim.ch
The Gasthaus Jägerheim is a family-run business in the hamlet of Ausserbinn. The guesthouse has 8 double rooms and the on-site restaurant serves traditional Valaisian fare that's a fresh interpretation to César Ritz's culinary legacy. Game is a speciality. Located in the Binn Valley, expect warm hospitality, fine cuisine and an excellent wine cellar.

Hotel Ofenhorn

Uf em Acher 1
Tel. 027 971 45 45
www.ofenhorn.ch
Open: 13 May to 23 October (2010); 18 December (2010) to 2 January (2011); culture evenings
A stay in this hotel becomes a journey through time, because the traditional Hotel Ofenhorn is steeped in history. Rooms, corridors and the dining room exude the spirit of the Belle Époque. The original furniture and decor from the period of the hotel's founding, still graces the interior spaces. There are wooden floors and the ceilings and walls are decorated in the Biedermeier and Art Nouveau styles. Each room is decorated differently. Four were lovingly restored as 'nostalgic rooms' and are reminiscent of the 19th century. Two have balconies with magnificent views

of the Ofenhorn and Weisshorn. Even the restaurant keeps to the traditional with its Valais specialities. The hotel was built in 1883 for English visitors and among its distinguished guests was Sir Winston Churchill who stayed there in 1897. It's a listed building and is included in 'Swiss Historic Hotels'. The hotel is an ideal base for touring and hiking in the wild, secluded Binn valley.

Brig

Hotel Victoria

Bahnhofstrasse 2
Tel. 027 923 15 03
www.hotel-victoria-brig.ch
The hotel is opposite the station and a popular meeting point. The brasserie and restaurant, Le Français, features local specialities and a good range of wines. It is within walking distance of Stockalper castle.

Hotel Ambassador

Saflischstrasse 3
Tel. 027 922 99 00
www.ambassador-brig.ch
A central three star hotel with five star service. This family run hotel is in a good, quiet location yet near the station and bus terminal. There are courteous and friendly staff and gourmet cuisine either in the splendid Art Deco Brasserie or the Hunting Room Restaurant. It has one of the best breakfasts in Brig and free parking.

Bürchen

Hotel Bürchnerhof

Ronalpstrasse 86
Tel. 027 934 24 34
www.buerchnerhof.ch
Part of the 'silence hotel' chain, this

YOUR KEY TO A SUCCESSFUL HOSPITALITY CAREER

César Ritz Colleges Switzerland is one of the world's leading institutions for hotel and tourism management. On our cosmopolitan campus you can benefit from traditional academic tutoring, paid internships and learn essential leadership skills. Study to Higher Diploma, Bachelor, Postgraduate Diploma and Masters levels or Culinary Arts. Enjoy personalized career planning from our dedicated career team.

Intakes throughout the year
We welcome new intakes in January, April, July and October. For more information on our full range of courses, please contact us on the address below.

Reserve a visit

It's the best way to find out what life as a César Ritz student is all about and whether a career in hospitality is for you. Do not hesitate to take advantage of our invitation, room and board are free!

César Ritz Colleges Switzerland – 1897 Le Bouveret – Switzerland – **www.ritz.edu** – admissions@ritz.edu – Tel. +41 24 482 82 82

is situated in a mountain village at 1500 metres and has stunning views. Its cuisine has various regional and seasonal specialities, and range of select wines. There is also a 200-metre indoor pool, children's pool and jacuzzi.

Champery

Art Boutique Hotel Beau Sejour
114 Reue du Village
Tel. 024 479 5858
www.beausejour.ch
Auberge Le Paradis
33 Route du Grand Paradis
Tel. 024 479 1167
www.grandparadis.ch

Champex-Lac

Hotel du Glacier
CH-1938 Champex-Lac
Tel. 027 782 6151
www.hotelglacier.ch
www.champex.info
www.flore-alpe.ch
This three star hotel is a real find! Established in 1895 by Paul Biselx, the hotel is now run by the fifth generation, Yves and his family. Ideal for families as everything is on the doorstep. Skiing is a short walk away, so is the lake with its boating in summer and there's an Alpine botanical garden on the sunny slopes of Mount Catogne. It's also on the classic trekking route, Tour de Mont Blanc.

Fiesch

Hotel des Alpes
Tel. 027 971 1506
www.des-alpes.ch

Fieschcralp

Hotel Eggishorn
Tel. 027 971 1444
www.hotel-eggishorn.ch

Gondo

Hotel Stockalperturm
Tel. 027 979 25 50
www.stockalpertum.ch
Once a warehouse, then a coaching inn but always a meeting place for people looking for adventure. William Wordsworth, stayed here twice – once on a walking tour and on another occasion with his sister, Dorothy. Built in 1670 by the Baron Kaspar von Stockalper who was a legendary figure in the history of Valais. Although you can't stay In his castle, you can experience a unique historical ambience behind the stone walls. Each of the 10 rooms has a modern but snug decor and offers incredible comfort with the combination of wood and stone. There is also a dormitory of 20 beds for groups. It's ideal for business meetings or team building activities as there are also seminar rooms. Its location on the Italian border makes it convenient as a touring centre for Italy or the Valais. The Valaisians do their shopping at the Saturday market in Domodossola – only 20 minutes by car – while the Italian lakes and Milan can be reached in over an hour.

Leukerbad

Mercure Bristol
Rathausstrasse 51
Tel. 027 472 75 00
www.mercure.com
A four star hotel with a personable atmosphere. Take the waters in style

in its private thermal bath, indoor pool and 2 outdoor pools. There is a fitness room, bio-sauna, a new spa with massage and beauty centre and restaurant. In line with innovation, the hotel also has a carnozet – a special Swiss cellar where you can enjoy traditional dishes like fondue, raclette and rösti with wine. Meeting and conference facilities are also available.

Hotel Grichting
Tel. 027 472 7711
www.hotel-grichting.ch
A four star family run hotel in a quiet location. The restaurant, La Terrasse, is known for its cuisine. There is also a saltwater pool and steam baths.

Les Sources des Alpes
Turftstrasse 17
Tel. 027 472 20 00
www.sourcesdesalpes.ch
A five star hotel with a gourmet Restaurant, La Malvoisie. An indoor and outdoor thermal bath, sauna, Turkish bath, solarium and fitness centre. A large choice of treatments and packages are available.

Lindner Hotels & Alpentherme
Dorfplatz
Tel. 027 472 10 00
www.lindnerhotels.ch
A four star hotel centrally located. Private thermal pools, sauna and spa. Underground connection between the hotel and the Lindner Alpentherme. Relax in the piano bar and lounge.

Lötschental

Hotel Bietschhorn und Nesthorn
Ried
Tel. 027 939 11 06
www.nest-bietsch.ch
Those who love mountains will adore this place. The doyen of the Golden Age of Mountaineering, Sir Leslie Stephen, who conquered the Bietschhorn stayed here. So did the young American climber, William Coolidge and his intrepid aunt, Miss Brevoort – a female mountaineer. The hotel is at the base of the Bietschhorn in Ried. It is cosy as can be with a library and in winter, a wood fire. Built in 1868, it is the oldest hotel in the Lötschental. It was renovated in 1986 and offers exceptional comfort in a family atmosphere, provided by its owners, Helene and Erwin Bellwald. The chef, Erwin Bellwald, has a creative cuisine which is complimented by seasonal dishes. The restaurant seats 66 people, the terrace 32 with a view of the Bietschhorn, On the first floor a stylish, quiet dining room is suitable for all sorts of celebrations. The hotel has 17 cozy rooms with impressive views. You can relax either in the sauna or sit in cosy lounges. The hotel boasts a new trendy sun terrace.

Hotel Edelweiss
Blatten
Tel. 027 939 13 63
www.hoteledelweiss.ch
Part of the 'silence' chain, Hotel Edelweiss is a family run establishment. It goes back three generations when Lukas Kalbermatten's grandfather sold his farm to open a hotel in 1968. His father was a pioneer in cross-country

4-star hotel with its own private thermal bath and spa with massage and beauty centre.

skiing in the early 1970s. Lukas himself gives free guided tours around the village including a visit to the village bakery, sawmill and the Walche, and tells you about the traditions and history. The hotel's situated in Blatten, the last village in the Lötschental, and until the 1950s was isolated as it had no road or cable car. It still retains its own character and is one of the most typical valleys in the Alps. Surrounded by trees, meadows, forests and mountains, the hotel is the place to relax and has been officially classified as 'Holiday and Hiking Hotel'. The bedrooms are tastefully furnished and come with or without a balcony. Some have disabled access. There are family bedrooms for 4 to 6 people that are offered at special group prices. A substantial breakfast buffet comes with the price of the room. The best quality products from the region are served either in the dining room or on the sunny terrace until 10 am. Guests can even grind their own muesli! The menus change three times a year to reflect the seasons. Children are also well catered for and there is a children's corner and a playroom. The use of the sauna and saunarium is included. The hotel is open all year round.

Hotel Fafleralp
Im Paradies
Fafleralp
Tel. 027 939 14 53
www.fafleralp.ch
The hotel is off the beaten track and is ideal for total rest and activities like cross-country skiing or hiking. The site is surrounded by majestic

summits with panoramic views of the Lötschental Valley. To ensure the freedom from stress and noise, there are no telephones or televisions in the rooms. The aim of the hotelier, Christian Henzen, his brother Pius and their sister, Aloysia Jeitziner is to make the guests feel at home. They succeed with their helpfulness and conviviality. Pius also acts as mountain guide and offers wellbeing treatments. The hotel has a restaurant, a self service area and offers banqueting facilities for weddings or conferences. During winter, luggage is transported from Blatten and the hotel is reached on foot.

Martigny

Hotel Forum
Avenue du Grand St.Bernard 72
Tel. 027 722 79 25
www.hotel-forum.ch
A three star hotel located near the old town or Bourg. It is known for its cuisine.

Mercure du Parc
Rue Marconi 19
Tel. 027 720 1313
www.hotelduparc.ch
A four star hotel situated in a large garden and not far from the station and the centre.

Münster

Hotel Croix d'or et poste
Tel. 027 974 15 15
www.hotel-postmuenster.ch
It is worth passing over the string of hotels along Goms in favour of the extraordinary Croix d'Or et Poste in Münster. It has provided hospitality to illustrious guests like Goethe and the Grand Duke, Karl August of Saxo Weimar-Eisenach, Edward Whymper who stayed twice and Monseigneur Ratti who became Pope Pius XI. The hotel, built in 1620, was the home for several generations of the noble family, von Riedmatten, who were prince-bishops in the Valais. The interior still reflects the 'supra Ecclesia' splendour of those days. The 21 rooms are all furnished in the rococo style and one even has a four-poster bed. Little touches have been added by the owners to increase the comfort of their guests. A tray for shoe-cleaning is outside each room and they provide a free taxi service between Oberwald and Niederwald. They also offer transportation of guests' luggage through the Swiss Rail baggage service. The restaurant's gastronomic cuisine has a new César Ritz menu every month. Banqueting facilities, large or small, are offered for weddings, business meetings and conferences.

St Gingolph

Hotel le Rivage
Tel. 024 482 70 30
www.rivage.ch
Situated directly on the shore of Lake Geneva, just a few metres from the French border
, the hotel offers absolute tranquillity. There are moorings for private boats, a landing stage for the boats which ply regularly between St-Gingolph and Geneva, Lausanne, Montreux, Villeneuve and other destinations. There is also an excellent restaurant.

A warm welcome is extended to our guests.
The hotel is the oldest and most traditional in the Lötschental.
Enjoy the seasonal dishes and our hospitality for which we are well known.

Helene and Erwin Bellwald.

Tel: 0041 939 1106
Website: www.nest-bieschhorn.ch

La Dame du Lac

Boat and Breakfast
Mailbox 37
1897 Le Bouveret
Tel. 079 301 98 93
www.ladamedulac.ch
Boat and breakfast is an original idea. Spend a night on a sailing boat in Bouveret harbour, sleep in a cabin to the accompaniment of lapping water. There is a choice of two sizes of sailing boat – Le Tonic 23 is ideal for a couple or a small family, while Le Grand Bleu, with its two cabins, caters either for a large family or a group of friends.

St Luc

Bella Tola

Tel 027 475 1444
www.bellatola.ch
The four star hotel reflects the lifestyle of the late 19th century. The current owners have enthusiastically set out to restore the guest rooms, the original dining room and lounges, to reflect the charms of a bygone age. It's a member of 'Swiss Historic Hotels'.

Hotel Weisshorn

Tel: 027 475 11 06
www.weisshorn.ch
Perched like an eagle's nest on a cragg, the hotel is at an altitude of 7,667 ft and has an impressive panorama. Since its opening in 1887, the Belle Epoque hotel has pampered its guests with excellent cuisine, sophisticated service and the best wines of the region. It can only be reached on foot, skis, mountain bike. Transport is provided for luggage. A sublime experience after a hike in summer or cross-country skiing and a

snow-shoe walk in winter!

Sierre
Coline de Daval
3960 Sierre
Tel. 027 458 45 15
www.collinededaval.ch
A bed and breakfast in a little castle situated in the middle of a vineyard. The rooms are decorated in an Art Nouveau style. Guests are spoilt by the breakfasts with home-made jams and juices as well as freshly baked bread with regional cheese and dried meat.

Hotel Terminus
Rue de Bourg 1
Tel. 027 455 1351
www.hotel-terminus.ch
The hotel is run by Didier de Courten who has an award-winning restaurant.

Simplon
Hotel Fletschhorn
3907 Simplon Dorf
Tel. 027 979 1138
www.hotelfletschhorn.ch
Run by the Escher family, the hotel has a homely atmosphere and good food.

Hotel Restaurant Grina
3907 Simplon Dorf
Tel. 027 979 1304
www.hotelgrina.ch
Romeo and Rita Arnold own the hotel and the cuisine is excellent.

Simplon Hospice
3907 Simplon
Tel. 027 979 13 22
www.gsbernard.ch
Founded in 1831 by the community of St Bernard, it provides accommodation in rooms or dormitories. Some guests use it as a retreat, others like climbers and walkers just spend a night.

Sion
Best Western Hôtel du Rhone
Rue du Scex 10,
Tel. 027 322 8291
www.bestwestern.com
A four star hotel situated in the centre of Sion.

Torgon
Hotel Restaurant Torgon
5 Rue de la Lanche
1899 Torgon
Tel. 024 481 15 71
www.torgon.ch
A boutique hotel providing all the accoutrement for a good stay – from beauty products in bathrooms to bathrobes, slippers, newspapers and magazines.

Hotel du Barrage
Grande Dixence
1987 Hérémence
tel. 027 281 13 22
www.hotel-barrage.ch
The hotel is at the foot of the Grande Dixence dam. It's ideal base if you want to enjoy the flora and fauna along the Ibex trail or visit the dam.
(www.grande-dixence.ch)

Climate
The Valais has little rainfall and over 300 sunny days a year. The temperatures vary according to altitude. It's not unusual to see snow covered peaks during a hot summer. Winters can be extremely cold with heavy snowfalls, while spring and autumn are moderate.

Concerts

Valaisians are very musical and concerts are held all over the canton including churches and chapels. There are shrovetide celebrations like carnivals where Guggenmusik is performed. More information can be found at www.fleigutaetscher.ch
In all instances, check with Tourist offices.

Currency

The Swiss Franc is the currency of the Swiss Federation.

Diplomatic Corps

British Embassy
Thunstrasse 50
3000 Bern 15
Tel. 031 359 77 00
www.britishembassy.ch

Irish Embassy
Kirchenfeldstrasse 68
Postfach 262
3000 Bern 6
Tel: 031 352 14 42/43
www.embassyofireland.ch

Canadian Embassy
Kirchenfeldstrasse 88
Postfach
3000 Bern 6
Tel. 031 357 32 00
www.canada-ambassade.ch

United States of America Embassy
Sulgeneckstrasse 19
Postfach
3007 Bern
Tel. 031 357 70 11
http://bern.usembassy.gov/

Driving Regulations

Right-hand side driving. Visitors need a sticker for driving on the motorways.

Electricity

The voltage in Switzerland is 220 volts, 50 Hz, and plugs have three points.

Emergency Medical Service

Ring 144 and the Cantonal rescue service will come to your aid anywhere on the mountains.
The service is free but tourists will have to pay for the helicopter or ambulance service. It's advisable to have accident insurance.

Entertainment for Children

Nature Reserve Pfyn-Finges
Postal case 65, 3970 Salgesch
Tel. 027 452 60 60
www.pfyn-finges.ch
This is the largest park in the Valais and encompasses 14 villages. There are a variety of special events for children. (A brochure is available.)

Pizza baking
Leukerbad tourism,
Tel. 027 472 71 71
www.leukerbad.ch
Children are introduced to the art of pizza baking. In winter, there's a special Swiss Snow Kids Village to entertain them including a Pinocchio lift.

Alpine Zoo
1923 Les Marécottes, postal case, 1922 Salvan
Tel. 027 761 15 62
www.zoo-alpin.ch
The zoo is 15 minutes by train from Martigny. Open all year round.

Be spoilt by an extraordinary hotel. Even a new César Ritz menu each month.

Hotel Croix d'or et poste

CH-3985 Münster
027 974 15 15
www.hotel-postmuenster.ch

Maze of Evionnaz
Labyrinth adventure, 1902 Evionnaz
Tel. 027 766 40 10
www.labyrinthe.ch
The largest maze in the world. More
than 50 games available for children,
as well as wall-climbing, mini golf and
a trampoline. Open all year round

Swiss Vapeur Parc
Route de la Plage 1897 Le Bouveret,
Tel. 024 481 44 10
www.swissvapeur.ch
The park is open from March to
November.

Happylandnew – fun fair
Rte du Foulon, 3977 Granges
Tel. 027 458 34 25
www.happylandnew.ch
Happylandnew is the largest theme
park in Switzerland.

Aquapark le Bouveret
Rte de la Plage, 1897 Le Bouveret,
Tel.024 482 00 00
www.aquapark.ch
'The Carribbean on Lake Geneva'.

Flag
The Valaisian flag is red and white with
red and white stars and a mixture of
red-white stars. It symbolizes the 13
districts in the canton.

Health
EU visitors are advised to have a
European Health Insurance Card (EHIC)
which is accepted in Switzerland

Helicopter
Air Zermatt 027 966 86 86
Air-Glaciers 027 329 1415.

For sightseeing or heliskiing.

Hiking
It's important to prepare before you set
out, for more information:
www.valrando.ch/hiking/tips/preparation.
php
The Valais is a paradise for hikers.
Below is a partial list of trails:

Lötschberg-Panoramaweg
Lauchernalp–Fafleralp
A high-level path on sunny Lötschental
slopes, through fragrant flower meadows
and forest. Stunning views into the
valley, impressive peaks and glacier
panorama. Bathe in the Schwarzsee
and read about Lötschental legends en
route. A classic hike.

Chemin des Bisses
Nendaz–Veysonnaz
Nendaz is a good place for hikes along
the suonen as there are a choice of
8. Enjoyable tour from Planchouet to
Veysonnaz, through flowery meadows
alongside the open channel of the
restored Grand Bisse de Vex.

Via Stockalper
Simplon Pass–Simplon Dorf
Descend on the south side of the
Simplon Pass through fascinating
Alpine landscape with Alp settlements
and hamlets to Simplon village. There is
a museum on the history of the pass in
Simplon village.

Suspension Bridge Belalp-Riederalp
Belalp–Riederalp
The Aletschji-Grünsee suspension
bridge was opened in July 2008.

LÖTSCHENTAL - THE MAGIC VALLEY
Lötschental - a wonderful experience in summer and winter
WWW.LOETSCHENTAL.CH
Lötschental - a wonderful experience in summer and winter
Lötschental
LAUCHERNALP

Over 30,000 keen hikers crossed the suspension bridge during the summer following its inauguration.

Aletsch Panorama
Bettmerhorn–Fiescheralp
Impressive views from Bettmerhorn summit station into the icy heart of the Swiss Alps Jungfrau-Aletsch UNESCO World Heritage site. There is a scenic cliff path over stone slabs to the Märjelensee lake. Over thousands of years, the glacier has shaped the magnificent high-Alpine landscape around the Jungfrau, Aletsch and Bietschhorn.

Champéry
Champéry Circlular
The Dents du Midi, the pristine and wild, undeveloped mountain massif between Val du Trient and Val d'Illiez is traversed in a circle via a 25-mile long trekking route. The tour consists of three to four day-long journeys, far from roads, trains and towns.

Eggerberg
Eggerberg-Lalden
The ridge path along the southern Lötschberg ramp from Hohtenn to Eggerberg/Lalden is one of Switzerland's best-known panorama routes and a classic for train fans, nature lovers and panorama addicts.

Websites for hikers:
www.Valrando.ch
http://www.wanderland.ch/en/routen_
etappen.cfm?id=317708
www.alptrekking.com
www.myswitzerland.ch
www.Valais.ch

Internet Information
www.valais.ch
www.myswitzerland.ch
www.valaisguide.co.uk

Mountain Guides
Suzanne Huesser
email:suzanne.huesser@bluewin.ch
There are many experienced mountain guides in the Valais and Suzanne Huesser is an exemplar of the group. A fully certified mountain guide of International Federation of Mountain Guide Associations (IFMGA), she has climbed most of the 13,200 ft (4,000 m) peaks in the Alps and has been up the Matterhorn 45 times.

Other Guides
http://www.4000plus-vs.ch/de/guides.html
A comprehensive list of guides can be found here.

Museums
www.valais.ch/en/Valais-CultureVS-
MuseumsVS-316426.html
There are over 50 museums in the Valais. They cover various subjects from Gallo-Roman artifacts in Martigny to vines and wine in Sierre and Salgesch to masks in Kippel, Lötschental and boats in St Gingolph. The website gives descriptions and all necessary information to most museums in the Valais. The principal museums are listed below:

Cantonal Museum of Fine Arts
CH-1950 Sion Tel. 027 606 46 90
The Museum exhibits both early and modern works of Valaisian artists.

Cantonal History Museum

CH-1950 Sion
Tel. 027 606 47 10
From the neolithic period (3,000 BC)
with anthropomorphous steles to
famous carved liturgical trunks of
the cathedral of Sion (13th century),
to Alp tourism and the industrial
transformation of the Valais with the
railway tunnels.

Cantonal Natural History Museum

CH-1950 Sion
Tel. 027 606 47 31
Scientific collections including 3500
rocks and minerals, 650 fossils, 2000
plants and 3500 animals. An inventory
of the Mammals of Valais is
in preparation.

Fondation Gianadda – Art and Archaeology in Martigny

CH-1920 Martigny
Tel. 027 722 39 78
The museum is renowned for
international art exhibitions and its
collection of 20th century sculptures. It
also has archaeological exhibits, vintage
cars and Leonardo da Vinci scientific
works. Open every day.

St Bernard Dog Museum

Rte du Levant 34 CH-1920 Martigny
Tel. 027 720 49 20
The St Bernard dogs were first
mentioned in 1707 and they became
a famous icon of mountain rescue with
their little flask of brandy on their collars.
The museum displays the entire history
and dogs are always on site.

Nightclubs

Dancing Masque de Bois

CH-1972 Anzère
Tel. 027 398 45 18

Alpfrieden

CH-3992 Bettmeralp
Tel. 027 927 22 32
www.alpfrieden.ch

Roxy Club

Route de l'Industrie 9
CH-1964 Conthey
Tel 079 315 16 92

Restaurant Dancing Happyland

Furkastrasse
CH-3984 Fiesch
Tel. 027 971 10 20

Courage Club

Rathausstrasse 32
CH-3954 Leukerbad
Tel. 027 472 20 30

Sphinx, Night Event SA

Rue de Bévignoux 12
CH-1920 Martigny
Tel. 027 722 88 18

Cabaret le Derby-Dome

Granges Thierry
Rue du Léman 45
CH-1920 Martigny
Tel. 027 722 15 76

La Cravache

CH-1911 Ovronnaz
Tel. 079 463 79 68 Bains de Saillon

Regional Nature Park Pfyn-Finges

Why not come along and discover the secrets of the natural landscape and culture of Valais, stock up on products from the region or treat yourself to a fantastic picnic in a fabulous spot? We will be happy to help make your stay in Valais something quite special.

We look forward to welcoming you!

The Nature and Landscape Centre provides information on the region and what it has to offer, all year round. We will be happy to advise you. For further information, including opening times, please contact us or visit our web page:

Tel. +41 (0)27 452 60 60 / Email admin@pfyn-finges.ch / Internet www.pfyn-finges.ch

La Locanda Attianésé Antonio
Route de la Gemmi
CH-3960 Sierre
Tel. 027 455 18 26

Five Roses
CH-3960 Sierre
Tel. 027 455 09 11

Trentequarante
Bernie Mix Sàrl
Rue de Lausanne 130
CH-1950 Sion
Tel. 027 346 30 41
www.trentequarante.ch

Le Pacha
Gaidon Stéphane
CH-1993 Veysonnaz
Tel. 079 424 97 17

Passports/Visas
www.myswitzerland.com/de/reisen/
reiseinformationen/einreise/passport-
visum.html
Travellers from the EU can also enter
with an identity card.

Parks and Nature Reserves
Pfyn-Finges
Postal case 65,
CH-3970 Salgesch
+41 (0)27 452 60 60
www.pfyn-finges.ch
This is the largest park in the Valais and
encompasses 14 villages.

Binn Valley
Römerbrücke
CH-3996 Binn.
Tel. +41 27 971 50 50
www.landschaftspark-binntal.ch
The area covers one of the richest

mineral deposits in the world.

Val d'herens
Rue Principale 13 –
CH-1982 Euseigne
027/281.28.15
www.valdherens.ch
There are nine villages that make up
the park including the remarkable Val
Ferret.

Nature Reserve Center Villa Cassel
Riederfurka 3987
Riederalp
Tel. 027 928 62
www.pronatura.ch/aletsch
The Aletsch forest has the oldest
stone pine trees in Switzerland and
sits alongside the Aletsch glacier.

Grangettes
www.vaudtourisme.ch
Although, this park is in the canton
Vaud, it's next door to Bouveret and
easy to reach. A breeding ground for
the great crested grebe.

Restaurants
A partial list is below:

Albinen
Wirtshaus Godswärgjistubu
Neben der Kirche
Tel. 027 473 21 66
www.godswaergjistubu.ch
God's Dwarf restaurant has an
ambience of a 17th century farmhouse.
A set four course meal, with vegetables
from their own garden, is delicious.
Closed on Tuesday and Wednesday.

The restaurant BRIAND, a family concern with lots of charm.

Located in the heart of the Torrent hiking and skiing area, next to the middle cable car station.

Torrentalp. 3955 Albinen • Tel: 027 470 1908 • website: www.restaurant-briand.ch

Restaurant Flaschen
Cable Car Station at Flaschen
Tel. 027 470 17 55
www.restaurant-flaschen.ch
Rene Briand surprises with his creative
cuisine at a ski station restaurant. Worth
a visit.

Restaurant Briand
Torrentalp
Tel. 027 470 19 08
www.restaurant-briand.ch
The restaurant is a second generation
family enterprise. Located in the heart
of the Torrent hiking and skiing area just
next to the middle cable car station.
A mountain restaurant which not only
offers a self-service restaurant but a
cosy Valaisian dining room. It also has
a large sun terrace with magnificent
views of the alps. The apple cake is
renowned.

Sunnublick restaurant/Pension
Tel. 027 473 13 87
www.sunnublick.ch
Seasonal dishes and local wines. The
garden terrace offers magnificent views
of the Rhone valley. Free wireless
connection in the pension.

Bouveret

Le Phare
Chemin du Vieux Port
Le Bouveret
Tel. 024 481 58 23
The restaurant has haute cuisine and
views from one of the prettiest lakeside
terraces. Highly recommended for the
seafood dishes for which it has won
awards

Champery

Le c21
Tel. 024 479 1550
www.centrechampery.ch
Surprising menu and innovative cuisine.

Ernen/Niederernen

Gommerstube
Tel. O27 971 29 71
www.gommerstuba.com
Rolf Gruber's creativity for new recipes
is endless and dishes are flavoured with
herbs from his own vegetable garden.
There is a large choice of the best
Valaisan wines. The terrace has a view
of the Eggishorn.

Ernen

St George
Tel. 027 971 11 28
www.stgeorg-ernen.ch
Klaus Leuneberger has had
international experience in the United
Arab Emirates and on the QEII. His
gourmet dishes are unconventional and
he uses only regional and bio products.
A special ambience is created by the
16th century building which was once a
nobleman's residence.

Tea Room
Mühlbachstrasse
Tel. 027 971 33 32
A cosy tea room with home-made
cakes and bread.

Leukerbad

Restaurant Bodmenstübli
Hamlet Bodmen
Tel 027 470 14 84
www.bdomenstuebli.ch
Valaisian cooking and regional wine
specialities. The Arolla pine dining

Come to Finhaut, Switzerland and have a blast from the past adventure!

JURASSIC JITTERS

The Emosson dam of Finhaut, towering at 1,200 metres, harbours one of the most stunning dinosaur tracks of Europe, a must see!
Come and behold breathtaking vistas of the Mont-Blanc and enjoy typical swiss hospitality dining on the roof top of the Valais!

GET ALL THE DETAILS HERE WWW.FINHAUT.CH
OR INFO@FINHAUT.CH / +41 27 768 12 78

room is tastefully decorated and has marvellous views from the panoramic terrace. Deckchairs and hammocks are available as well as a children's playground.

Restaurant Weidstübli
Tel. 027 470 35 58
www.weidstuebli.ch
Situated in the centre of several hiking tracks. In winter there is folk music and toboggan rides down. The building has a panoramic terrace.

Lötschental
Kippel
Restaurant Dorfkeller
Tel. 027 939 1626
www.restaurant-dorfkeller.ch
Local dishes and wines.

Wiler
Restaurant Lonza
Tel. 027 939 1231
Mob. 079 751 1023
www.restaurant-lonza.ch
Ambros Henzen is the third generation chef who runs the restaurant. Whereas his grandfather would serve a meat and vegetable soup as a main course, he offers a menu of local fresh bio meat, pasta and vegetarian meals. There's also an unusual dish of black neck kid sausage or casserole. For seasoning pasta, he grates Belper Knolle cheese instead of parmesan. A speciality is the dessert of Chächlini, a dark bread cake. He also sells a range of natural foods and beauty products.

Martigny
Chez Pierre
Rue de Bourg 51

Tel. 027 720 6172
www.die-restaurants.ch
Good ambience and food.

La vache qui vole
Place centrale 2B
1920 Martigny
Tel. 027 722 38 33
www.lavachequivole.ch
A bar and restaurant with a zany flying cow emblem. Classic dishes include Tagliatta de filet de boeuf and Tartare de boeuf coupé au coupeau.

Nendaz
Restaurant Mont-Rouge
Tel. 079 634 4962
www.mont-rouge.ch
A cosy restaurant with a refined cuisine that is inspired by the local produce. There's a large shady terrace with a beautiful view over the Alps.

Ried Brig
Hotel-Restaurant Chavez
Simplonstrasse 27
Tel. 027 923 1308
www.hotelchavez.ch
The restaurant with a quaint wood-panelled Chavez dining room takes its name from Geo Chavez, the first aviator to cross the Alps in 1910. A dining room is decorated with Chavez memorabilia. A bio food menu is served.

Sierre
Château de Villa
Rue St Catherine (near Château Mercier)
Tel. 027 455 18 96
www.chateaudevilla.ch
The ideal place to eat Valaisian specialties, specially Raclette, dried

LEUKERBAD.CH
Sport and thermal bathing
Enjoy Leukerbad during 365 days
with the whole family
ALBINEN – INDEN – VAREN
LEUKERBAD
Leukerbad Tourismus, Rathaus, CH-3954 Leukerbad
Telefon +41 (0)27 472 71 71, Fax +41 (0)27 472 71 51, www.leukerbad.ch, info@leukerbad.ch

meat and brisolée (roasted chestnuts).

Didier de Courten
Hotel Terminus
Rue de Bourg 1
Tel. 027 455 1351
www.hotel-terminus.ch
The top chef in the Valais, Didier de Courten, runs an excellent restaurant in the historic Terminus hotel. Enjoy the pleasures of a creative and delicious meal, refined service and a good choice of wines. Served in a contemporary dining room or on the patio under the shade of plane trees.

Sion
L'Enclos de Valère
Rue des Châteaux 18
1950 Sion
Tel. 027 323 32 30
www.enclosdevalere.ch
The Enclos de Valère is situated below the castles of Valeria and Tourbillon in the old town. It has a terrace with a view and a gourmet menu.

La Sitterie
Route du Rawyl 41
Tel. 027 203 2212
www.lasitterie.ch
Jacques Bovier is enthusiastic about creative cuisine. Guests can enjoy a luxuriant garden.

Au Cheval- Blanc
Rue du Grand Pont 23
Tel. 027 322 18 67
www.au-cheval-blanc.ch
The restaurant is situated in the heart of the historic town. Seafood is a speciality.

Le Coq en Pâté/Supersaxo
Passage Supersaxo
Tel 027 346 22 33
www.coqenpate.ch
The restaurant has a splendid ambience as it's situated in the Supersaxo Mansion. The dining room is renowned for its ceiling. The cuisine is classic and creative with wines from the local vineyards.

Sion-La Muraz
Relais de Mont d'Orge La Muraz
Tel. 027 395 33 46
www.ricou.ch
Bernard Ricou offers gourmet cuisine in the French tradition. Try the trilogy – a dish which contains three variations of the same meat or fish. A favourite of Oskar Freysinger, author and politician.

St Leonard
Buffet de la gare
ave. de la gare 35
Tel. 027 203 4343
www.buffetdelagare-st-leonard
The small station at St Leonard is the last place you would expect to find a good restaurant. It was started by Madame Josette Bovier-Salamin's grandfather, Ernst Bovier, who had a buvette that served only wine and other beverages. Soon he transformed Buffet de la Gare into something much more where typical local dishes were served alongside some specialities. But it was a place of encounters because on Sundays, you could also dance. The family has prided itself on conviviality and the moment you cross the threshold, you are treated equally and with respect, irrespective of who you are and how you are dressed.

CHANDOLIN
GRIMENTZ
ST-LUC
SIERRE
VERCORIN
ZINAL

sierre anniviers
VALAIS WALLIS SWITZERLAND

Gastronomic
Journey

Valais
les Alpes-Source

From CHF 69.-/Pers.*

Wine tasting, typical meal of the Valais = CHF 69.-/pers.
Wine tasting, typical meal of the Valais, one night in ***hotel = CHF 164.-/pers.

+41 848 848 027   www.sierre-anniviers.ch/gastronomy

* indicative prices

ATELIER GRAND   Photo © photo-genic.ch

Consequently, the clientele who come regularly have made friends among themselves as well as with Madame. She knows of their table preferences and likes and dislikes. When you come here expect to be surprised because the ambience and decor could be that of a Parisian restaurant. The cuisine is Mediterranean with seasonal dishes and vegetables from Madame's own garden are used. Do try the wine as her husband won a silver medal for his vintage. A screen divides the restaurant from the little bistro which has a separate menu with reasonably priced fine dishes. Madame's daughter – a photographer – is also interested in the restaurant. So there will be a fourth generation at the Buffet de la Gare.

The restaurant is open from Wednesday morning until Sunday evening. It's advisable to book a table specially at the weekend.

St Luc

Hôtel Bella-Tola
Tel. 027 475 14 44
www.bellatola.ch
The French restaurant is in the winter garden of the Belle Epoque Bella-Tola Hotel. It offers cuisine using fresh market produce.

St Maurice

Restaurant Lafarge
Place de la Gare
Tel. 024 485 13 60
www.lafarge.ch
A unique establishment, part elegant haute cuisine dining, part casual and convivial local pub.

The Swiss Alpine Club
Mountain Huts

The Swiss Alpine Club (SAC) huts are open all year round and two thirds of them have simple meals and beverages. Book in advance. Brochures can be ordered online by info@sac-cas.ch or www.sac-cas.ch
The Monte Rosa Hut is the most modern and sophisticated mountain hut in the world. It lies high above Zermatt at the foot of the Dufour Summit at an altitude of 9,514 ft.

Shopping

The Valais is a Catholic Canton and shops are closed on Sunday. The exceptions are bakeries and petrol stations.
The most popular buys are Alpine cheese and dried meat. Eggs butcher in Reckingen, Goms has been awarded several medals for its dried meat and cheese & meh, Turtmann has won an award for raclette cheese.

Albinen

Toepferhuus
Tel 027 473 21 60
www.toepferhuus.ch
A pottery shop where you can buy stoneware and porcelain. It's run by Ursula Fattorini, a ceramic artist.

Binn

Minerals and crystals can be bought in Binn. There are courses in mineralogy as well as excursions in the Binn valley. Tel. 027 971 45 47

COME, SEE AND STAY

Conthey

Fromagerie la Grenette.
Route Cantonale 28.
Tel. 027322 2903
www.la-grenette.ch
The best cheesemonger in the Valais.
Adrian Rudaz has a range of over 250
cheeses including 50 from the Valais.
He complements the superb range with
sauces for fondues, dried meat and
sausages and other regional products.
There is also a branch in Sion.

Gondo

Hotel Stockalperturm
Tel. 027 979 25 50
www.stockalperturm
Here you can buy smuggler's back
baskets, filled with products of the
region. They also offer courses in gold
panning.

Lötschental

Wooden carved masks can be bought
in Wiler, Blatten, Ried and Kippel.
There are also courses in model mask
making. Ring Lötschental Tourismus for
more information. Tel. 027 938 88 88

Martigny

The Morand distillery shop
Place de Plaisance
Martigny.
Tel. 027 722 2036
www.morand.ch
It all started with Louis Morand who
improved the monk's recipe of the
Grand Saint-Bernard liqueur which the
famous dogs wore around their necks
when they rescued people lost in the
snow. André Morand took the English
Williams pear and turned it into the
incomparable brandy, Williamine, which

soon became a cult Swiss gift. His
great-grandson, Julien, has followed
the tradition of innovation with his
range of 'Douce de brandies'. With
less alcohol and sugar, he has started
a trend among the younger generation
who like the apricot, quince and pear
flavours. The Genevans like a 50-50
mix of the two sorts of Williamine. The
Morand distillery shop has a range of
fruit brandies like pear, quince, apricot,
apple, raspberry, plum and cherry as
well as the Grand St Bernard liqueur,
absinthe and syrups. In addition, it
has a remarkable selection of whiskies
and jams. The miniature bottles make
ideal gifts.

Goms

Obergesteln
Bahnhofstrasse 5
Tel. 079 381 62 23
The shop sells unusual ornaments
made from glass objects. The artist
is the local parish priest who, with his
housekeeper, run the shop.

Ried Brig

Schnitzerei und Giesserei Zennklusen
Simplonstrasse 55
Tel. 027 923 61 75
Wood carved objects such as
reliefs, plates, clocks, crucifixes and
sculptures. A carved wine bottle is an
unusual present.

Salgesch

Fructum Vitis
Heidi Kuonen-Goetz
Littenstrasse 12
Tel. 078 851 35 44
www.vinotherapy.ch
Various grapeseed products can be

Le Buffet de la Gare

"Once over her threshold, Madame Josette Bovier-Salamin
treats her clientele like friends.

A fourth generation restaurant where everything is
superb - ambiance, decor, the vegetables from her own
garden and her husband's prize-winning wine.

A trésor worth visiting.

Weekends are busy, so book ahead."

Le Buffet de la Gare,
35, Av. de la Gare - CH-1958 St-Léonard
www.buffetdelagare-st-leonard.ch

found here or at the Wine and Vine Museum of Salgesch.

Sierre

Fondation Rainer Maria Rilke
Maison Courten
Rue du Bourg 30
Tel. 027 456 26 46
www.fondationrilke.ch
A bookshop with English volumes on Rainer Maria Rilke's life and works.

The Manor Department Store
Rue de Sion
Tel. 027 451 1699.
Situated on the outskirts of Sierre, this is a popular shopping venue. It has a food hall, restaurant and other general departments.

Sion

The best shopping centre in the Valais is in Sion and the top patisserie in the Valais measures up to anything you can find in Paris. It's a great place to see the chic Sedunoise and while away the time.

Turtmann

Cheese und Meh
Kantonstrasse 12
Tel. 027 932 2121
www.cheesundmeh.ch
The local dairy farmers established this cheesemonger. The products are special as they are made from the milk of Alpine pastures. Raclette is a famous Valasian cheese which is scraped onto a plate as it melts. It's unpasteurised and eaten with potatoes. Hobel cheese is peeled in thin slices and is ideal to have with an aperitif.

Turtmanntal, Oberems

Madelaine Lötscher
Ahorn
Tel. 027 932 1248
Mob. 079 791 7743.
www.kraeuterhexlein.ch
AKA the 'Herb Witch', Lötscher grows some 142 herbs in her fields. Her handmade products include teas, creams, oils, syrups, wine and vinegar.

Visperterminen

Handarbeitsstube
Tel. 027 946 18 15 / 079 542 55 02
Handmade woollen items such as knitted bracelets and crochet can be found here

Vollèges

Route de Bagnes Etiez
Tel. 027 785 1040
A wonderful cheesemonger.

Skiing

Tel: 027 327 3570.
www.valaisskicard.ch
The Valais is a skiers' paradise. Ski stations are commonplace but remember the cost can be less than half at a lesser-known resort, the skiing conditions just as good and the queues shorter. For enthusiastic skiers, the Valais skicard is hands-free and allows entry to 54 regions and 4 thermal baths.

Thermal baths
Brigerbad

Thermalbad Brigerbad
Tel. 027 948 48 48
www.brigerbad.ch
The largest open-air swimming pools in Switzerland with a grotto pool, the

DISTILLERIE MORAND SHOP

PLACE DE PLAISANCE IN MARTIGNY

MONDAY TO FRIDAY : 8:30 TO 12:00 / 13:30 TO 18:30

SATURDAY : CLOSED AT 5 PM

longest alpine slide (597 ft), an Olympic swimming pool and turbulent wave pool.

Lavey
Les Bains de Lavey
Route des Bains 48
CH-1892
Tel. 024 486 1555
www.lavey-les-bains.ch
Situated on the plain, there are two outdoor pools and one indoor pool. They are the warmest thermal waters in Switzerland.

Leukerbad
Leukerbad Tourismus
Rathausstr. 8
Tel. 027 472 71 7
www.leukerbad.ch
Known since Roman times, 3.9 million litres of warm water flow daily into 22 thermal baths (open air and indoor pools). It's the biggest thermal bath and wellness resort in the Alps.

Ovronnaz
Office du Tourisme
Tel. 027 306 42 93
 www.ovronnaz.ch
The thermal bath centre, Thermalp les Bains has got 3 thermal pools and offers a versatile wellness programme.

Saillon
Office du tourisme
Rte du centre thermal
Tel. 027 743 11 88
www.saillon.ch
Three outdoor swimming pools together with a wellness complex.

Val D'illiez
Tel. 024 476 80 40
www.thermes-parc.com
An outdoor swimming pool in the region of 'Porte du Soleil' with a charming restaurant and a terrace.

Time Zones
Standard time zone: Central European Time. The local time in Switzerland is always GMT + 1 hour.

Tipping
At restaurants, service is included in the bill.
Ski Instructors: generally CHF 50.00 per person in the ski group following a week's lessons.
Chalet staff: generally CHF 50.00 – 100.00 for the service of the apartment is appreciated

Transport
The Valais is easily accessible for tourists either through the airports of Zurich or Geneva and then by car or train along Lake Geneva or through the tunnels. The quickest way is via Zurich to Kandersteg where there's a car transporter through the Lötschberg tunnel to Goppenstein. There are good connections throughout the Valais with the train and yellow postautos even to remote villages.

Free Bike rental
Reservations : www.valaisroule.ch
Free bikes are available for four hours from June to October at the following places:
Portvalaisroule, Monthey, Saint-Maurice, Fully, Sion, Sierre, Gampel, Leuk, Raron, Visp and Brig-Glis/

Naters. A 20.00 CHF deposit and ID or passport required.

Cable cars

www.bestofsnow.ch/transport/bergbahnen/wallis/mitglieder.html.
There are 56 cable cars in the canton with various facilities at the top. Two cableways operate in Leukerbad, the Gemmi and the Torrent

Leukerbad and the village of Albinen have extensive facilities.

The Gemmi cableway

This cableway takes you up to Gemmi pass (7,700 ft) where you can enjoy panoramic views from the hotel and restaurant.

The Torrent cableway

This offers you two routes up to the Torrent. The first from Leukerbad directly up to the top at Rinderhütte (7,709 ft), where you'll find a restaurant with panoramic views, a ski shop and a dormitory that sleeps 50. You have a choice of three routes to go down and ski lift or chair lifts to go up. For experienced skiers, there is a 'zigzag' on the descent. The other route up is from Albinen-Flaschen. The first part takes you to the middle station (6,299 ft) where you find restaurants including the Alpengruss with a dormitory, and the Briand which is next to it. From there you may wish to hike up to Rinderhütte or take the second stage of the cable car up.

Trekking Guides

Peter Salzmann
Fuelagasse 2
CH-3930 Visp
Tel. +41 (0) 79 680 14 67
An excellent guide.

For other guides try:
www.weinwanderungen.ch
www.alpevents.ch
The best source for other trekking guides are the Tourist offices in the Valais.

Wines

There are some 300 wine cellars in the Valais. (Refer to Valais Guide website. www.valaisguide.co.uk) The best way to get good wine is to buy directly from the producer. Besides the AOC certificate, there are further marks of quality such as the Grand Cru, the Charte Grain Noble Confidentiel and UVEV. (www.grainnoble.ch) and www.uvev.ch/membres.asp?l=1)

The first weekend in September the Vinea Association organizes Switzerland's largest open-air wine fair. Visitors are issued with a tasting passport and a glass, and can taste about 1,200 Swiss wines.
www.vinea.ch

www.vinsduvalais.ch
An English website that promotes Valais winegrowers.
www.cheminduvignoble.ch
The Valais wine route in German and French.
One is spoilt for choice in the Valais and only some wineries are used as exemplars. A partial list is given below:

Hike and ski to your heart's content in delightful alpine landscapes.

Four restaurants, ski shop, accommodation and giant scooters.

Torrent skiing and hiking pass offers.

Torrent's cable cars operate from Leukerbad and Albinen.

Adrian Mathier et Fils

Bahnhofstrasse 50
3970 Salgesch
Tel:027 455 7575
www.mathier.ch
(See Diego Mathier, Crown Prince of
Valasian Wine)

Chanton Weine

Kantontrasse 70
CH-3930 Visp
Tel.027 946 21 53
www.chanton.ch
Josef-Marie Chanton is a pioneer
of wine and has revived all the old
grape varieties grown in the Valais.
He first started with Lafnetscha, then
followed with Himbertscha, Gwäss,
Plantscher, Resi and Eyholzer Red. Of
these, Lafnetscha is the only authentic
Valaisian wine which is characterised by
a low alcohol content and a high acidity.
It's ideal as an aperitif and is a good
accompaniment for cheese, sauerkraut,
onion cake and crustaceans. Eyholzer
red is its counterpart and is a light
wine, almost a rosé. All Chanton
wines, according to Josef-Marie, are
the product of nature and do not need
unnatural means in order to grow.

Chappaz Marie-Thérèse

Ch. de Liaudise 39
CH-1926 Fully
Tel. 027 746 35 37
Mobile 079 636 49 87
www.chappaz.ch
(See Queen of Valaisian Wine)

Cave du Vidomne

Rue du Prieuré 8
CH-1955 St-Pierre-de-Clages
Tel. 027 306 2780

Mob. 079 206 9352
www.Chamoson
Meinrad and Catherine Gaillard produce
a brilliant range of prizewinning red
wines all aged in wood. Of these
Bâton Rouge is the most celebrated
and has a nose of very ripe fruit, more
like jam. It's ample and rich in the
mouth with a good structure and the
tannins are smooth and silky. But its
history is extraordinary because such
a wine would be certainly banned
in Italy. The reason is that they have
planted two grape varieties – Barbera
and Sangiovese – in the Valais which
produce the cheap Italian wine and
expensive Chianti respectively. It was a
gamble but Meinrad Galliard, who's a
true professional, focused on top quality
wines and won through. The blend of
these varieties in a different terroir have
proved to be a great success.

Their winemaking follows traditional
lines. After ten days of separate
maceration, the two varieties are put
in the same 450-litre oak barrel where
they remain for four years. They wait
a further four months after bottling
for the wine to recover. Their other
prizewinners include the Modus Vivendi
range of Syrah, the Assemblage and
the dry Chardonnay, Pinot Noir de
Chamoson and the sweet dried-on-the
vine Johannisberg, Timothyus One.

Charles Bonvin Fils

1950 Sion
Tel:027 203 4131
info@charlesbonvin.ch
www.charlesbonvin.ch
Charles Bonvin Fils was established
in 1858 and is the oldest winery in

Premium Swiss wines.
Spectacular vineyards
to visit!
BONVIN
les Domaines
Charles Bonvin Fils SA I Sion I Switzerland I www.charlesbonvin.ch

the Valais. It celebrated its 150th anniversary in 2008 with a re-creation of its red vintage 1858 which won the London gold medal in 1862. The wine is a blend of Cornalin and Syrah and is produced with the same methods used in the 19th century. The fermentation is carried out with the skin and it's mixed by hand in oak barrels and left unfiltered. The 1858 is a classy wine limited to 1858 bottles and 150 magnums. A deep, clear cherry red with fruity notes and a peppery aftertaste. Fleshy in the mouth with beautiful tannic qualities. A good accompaniment to meat, game and all kinds of cheeses.

What sets the winery apart from others in the Valais is that it owns the finest vineyards such as the Clos du Château, the Domaine Brûlefer, both near Sion, on the south facing steep slopes of the Rhone valley. Among the classics of the company are Fendant 'Domaine Brûlefer' and the spicy Dôle 'Clos du Château' prized by connoisseurs. They also have most of the ancient local varieties of the Valais like Petite Arvine, Amigne, Humagne and Cornalin. André Darbellay who is a successor to the four generations of the Bonvin family carries on the hallowed tradition. In the UK, Bonvin wines are served at 'Bettys', the Swiss-founded tea rooms in Harrogate, Yorkshire. www.bettys.co.uk

C. Varonier & Söhne

Hauptstrasse 4
3953 Varen
Tel: 027 473 1016
Mob: 078 610 9164
www.varonier.ch

Andy Varonier is the third generation in the traditional family winery. He's unique in the Valais as he has a British oenologist, Jamie McCulloch. They work well together and their Pfyfoltru AOC 2009 won a gold medal in the Le Mondial du Pinot Noir which is organised by VINEA. It's a remarkable achievement for a small winegrower as some 1,100 wines from 21 countries competed. The chalky soil of their vineyards in Varen are well suited to Pinor Noir grape variety.

Andy Varonier's philosophy on wine is to get a good balance between the fruit and the wood. It's important for the character of the wine to be prominent and to ensure that the wooden barrel doesn't predominate. Rather than two years, their wine is kept in the oak barrels for only four to six months.

They maintain that the Swiss wines are as good as the French but as most of the production is sold domestically rather than exported, the British are unaware of their superb quality. In fact, they compare well with the great wines from Burgundy as both regions lie at the same latitude – but the Valais wines have the edge because of their sunnier climate. Jamie McCulloch, originally from Stirling in Scotland, is quite at home with wine and whisky. In the past, the Highland chieftains always had a French connection as they traded whisky for wine.

Diroso Weinatelier

bei der Kirche
CH-3946 Turtmann
Tel. 027 032 3303

LES FILS DE CHARLES FAVRE
La petite maison des grands vins
Collection F
AOC VALAIS
SYRAH
ELEVÉE EN FÛT DE CHÊNE
LS DE CHARLES FAVRE SION
Fendant de la Dame de
PETITE ARVINE
Favi
Assemblage de Cépages Rouges
LA PETITE MAISON
LES GRANDS VINS
SYRAH
Les Fils de Ch. Favre SA / Av. de Tourbillon 29 / 1951 Sion Tél. 027 327 50 50
www.favre-vins.ch

www.diroso.ch
Hans-Peter Baumann who was once a banker began his career as winegrower when he married his wife Irene. She came from Visperterminen and under the Valaisian Inheritance law gained 700 square metres of vineyards. The law ensures that the parents' possessions are divided equally among their offspring and has accounted for over 20,000 smallholders in viticulture. Hans-Peter Baumann produces almost 30 varieties of wines in his five hectares of vineyards which is spread widely from Visperterminen to Sierre. However, he's innovative in his approach and has pioneered the grape varieties that are resistant to fungus. Muscat blue is an example of a resistant root stock and is a good table grape that produces a rosé wine with a bouquet of mango, quince and orange aromas. Such root stocks obviate the use of fungicides which require regular spraying. (English winegrowers have turned to the white Seyval blanc grapes for the same reason.)

Diroso Weinatelier is unique in two other ways. It offers the hobby winemakers an analysis service to create a better balanced wine. A common complaint is that the wine causes headaches which is due to the presence of histamines. It also has an ultimate present for the wine buff. For 300 CHF a year, you can own a row of grapevines that produces six bottles of your own labeled wine. This entitles you to work in the vineyard for a couple days under Hans-Peter Baumann's guidance. His two sons, Diego and Roman, also participate in the winery.

Giroud Vins

Route de Nendaz 1
CH-1950 Sion
Tel. 027 205 74 74
www.giroud-vins.ch
A mammoth building houses a wine cellar, a shop with over 500 bottles, including wines from abroad, a wine tasting area and reception, and conference rooms. The top of the range is the blend Constellation with Syrah, Humagne Rouge, Cabernet Franc, Cabernet Sauvignon and Cornalin. Petite Arvine from Chamoson is aromatic and vibrant and Moscato and Brut de Brut are good sparkling wines.

Jean-René Germanier
Balavaud

Route Cantonale 285
1963 Vétroz
Tel. 027 346 12 16
www:jrgermanier.ch
Urbain Germanier was a carpenter who turned his hand to winegrowing in 1896 and his grandson, Jean-René, proudly continues the tradition with his nephew Gilles Besse. Both oenologists, they knew that the terroir gives a strong identity to the wine. They chose the Syrah grape, with its long maturing character, to thrive on the sun-drenched slopes and in the slatey soil with its layered river and glacier sediments.

The first vintage of the top quality red wine was made in 1995 and called Cayas, a broken stone in the local patois. The yield was limited and produced more concentrated grapes. It is more fruity and spicy compared with the Syrah grown in the lower Rhone

Disarming

**Whatever the occasion or whatever the celebration:
We have the perfect wine.
Vins des Chevaliers – a Wine for Life.**

vins des chevaliers sa / varenstrasse 40 / 3970 salgesch, switzerland
t +41 027 455 28 28 / www.chevaliers.ch

in France. The late harvest and the different temperatures of cool nights and warm days gave the wine a broad aromatic palate. It's ideal to drink after five to seven years.

There is also the white Amigne for which Vétroz is renowned. It's available in the Grand Cru, the Classique or the sweet Mitis and the symbol of bees are used to designate the degree of sweetness.

Les Fils de Charles Favre SA

Av. de Tourbillon 29
CH-1951 Sion
Tel. 027 327 50 50
www.favre-vins.ch
A member of the vintner association of Sion, Favre is situated in the centre of town. The showroom is smart and yet casual with displays of its popular brands such as Dame de Sion, Hurlevent, Collection F and Favi. The Pinot noir of the range Hurlevent is an elegant, harmonious and balanced wine. Full-bodied, it acquires maturity a year after bottling and goes well with terrines, lamb, rabbit, poultry and cheese. The Dame de Sion is a Fendant, an aperitif wine par excellence. It has the typical qualities of a great white wine from the Valais. Dry, refined and fruity with a touch of elegance. A good accompaniment to raclette, fondue and cheese dishes. The wine is named after Hanny Favre, a grande dame, who was the first Valaisan woman to be a member of the Union of Wine Merchants.

Maye & Fils Simon

Rue de Collombey 3
CH-1955 St-Pierre-de-Clages
Tel. 027 306 41 81
www.simonmaye.ch
Jean-François and his brother Axel Maye run the winery which is well known for the old Syrah vines. The splendid wine is grown in the gravelly soil of Prés des Pierres terroir and is matured for 20 months, 12 of which are spent in a barrel.

Provins Valais

Rue de l'Industrie 22
1950 Sion
Tel. 084 066 6112
www.provins.ch
Chandra Kurt is an extraordinary wine person: she is a prominent wine journalist, an author of wine stories, a consultant on wine to an airline and has her own brand which is sold in the UK. But it's understandable if your father, Fred Kurt, was a famous zoologist. She draws a parallel between wine and art. Many of the winemakers are artists and their products are inestimable. She gives an example of Dirk Niepoort from the Douro valley in Portugal who's a complete artist – from new wine combinations to labelling. She herself teamed up with Madeleine Gay, the oenologist at Provins Valais, Switzerland's largest winery, to create her own range of wine. The idea is to launch the unknown grape varieties of the Valais such as Heida, Amigne, Humagne blanche and Humagne rouge, globally. Her own favourite wine, which is a biodynamic vintage from Burgundy, is Lalou Bizet's Domaine Leroy. It gives her goosebumps and

energizes her so much that when she's finished drinking it, she's totally exhausted. The Chandra Kurt Collection is available from Harrods, London. www.txb-finewines.com

René Favre & Fils

John & Mike Favre
Rte de Collombey 15
1955 - St-Pierre-de-Clages 15
Tel. 027 306 3921
079 291 3917 or 079 257 7053
Email. renefavrevin@chamoson.ch
 www.petite-arvine.ch

John and Mike Favre run their father René's winery which was founded in 1979. Both brothers are oenologists and have panache which is displayed in their lifestyles and wines. John, with his wicked, pirate ponytail and Mike, who roars off on his Harley Davidson 1938 flathead or Ducatti 999 to clear his mind. Their high quality list features Red Pickup and Blue Bike blends, bottles which are sealed stylishly with wax and the most expensive half case of six Honorables sells for 450 CHF to customers in Texas and New Mexico. The Red Pickup is an assemblage of Syrah, Merlot and Diolonoir which is remarkably rich and complex. The Blue Bike which is partly aged in a barrel is a blend of Sauvignon, Johannisberg, Chardonnay and Petite Arvine. Mike is proud of the Petite Arvine which originates from a 40-year-old vine and undergoes no malolactic fermentation to maintain its crisp acidity, soft fulness and complexity. There are two other fine white wines like Chardonnay Rouge de Honte which is vinified like a red wine and the award-winning Johannisberg. A top of the line red is Renommée St-Pierre which is a Pinot Noir that is matured several months in wood. The winery has a boutique which sells accoutrement for wine buffs as well as unusual items like felt handbags, sunglasses cases – all with grape motifs.

Rouvinez Vins

Colline de Géronde
3960 Sierre
Tel. 027 452 2245
www.rouvinez.com

The winery's early days were associated with the well-drained moraine hillside, the Colline de Géronde which gave its name to the Pinot Noir that was a gold medal winner at the 2009 Grand prix du Vin Suisse.

Vins des Chevaliers

Varenstrasse 40
3970 Salgesch
Tel. 027 455 2828
www.chevaliers.ch

The winery, which celebrates its 75th anniversary in 2011, was the first to bottle their wines under the appellation Salquenen. It adopted the logo of the Maltese knight and the Dôle des Chevaliers was the most popular brand in the country. The winery is located in the 'wine village of Switzerland', Salgesch/Salquenen, it revitalised the old Valais grape varieties and was among the first to introduce the Grand Cru. It has won several awards and its Chevalier Rouge (a blend of five different Valaisian grapes) was awarded Best Swiss Wine of the year 2008. Vins des Chevaliers has a long tradition in exporting to countries like Germany, Japan and most recently to China. The remodelled estate and wine tasting area is also worth a visit.

Patrick Z'Brun the idealistic owner and experienced mountaineer has launched a new brand, the 'Sherpa' wine. It's a red assemblage of Pinot Noir and Humagne Rouge. The Pinot Grape, partly maturing in oak casks, lends the wine strength and vigour. Humagne Rouge, with its soft tannins, delivers a fruity bouquet giving the wine its character. An eloquent and harmonious wine.

The Sherpa Wine tells the story of a particular Everest Expedition. It's in honour of the Himalayan Sherpas. Two Swiss Francs per bottle are donated for the Swiss Sherpa-Project, a foundation created by Patrick Z'Brun to train Sherpas to become recognized mountain guides
www.swiss-sherpa.ch

Wine tasting centres
The centres are open 7 days a week.
Fol'terres Agritourism Paviilion - Fully
Tel. 027 746 13 13
Mobile. 076 496 19 50
www.folterres.ch

Leytron Wine-tasting centre
L' Oenothèque des Bains
Route de Riddes 40
Leytron
Tel. 027 307 13 30
www.oeno.ch

La Verre a Pied – Sion
Av.Grand-Pont 40,
Tel. 027 321 13 13
www.sionpassion.ch

Swiss Wine Fair Sierre.

Villa Chateau Sierre
L'Oenothèque du Château de Villa
Tel. 027 456 24 29
www.chateaudevilla.

Weather
Before going on an outing in the mountains it is always advisable to check the weather conditions of the day.

http://www.valais.ch/de/weather.cfm
www.meteosuisse.ch

a) *Guided Tours in Leuk:* www.leuk.ch
Explore the historic town of Leuk: the charnel house, its castles and narrow alleys.
Every Tuesday, 14:30 h (July-Sept.)

b) *Art:* www.galleriagraziosagiger.ch & www.schlossleuk.ch
Contemporary art from Switzerland and foreign countries.

c) *Vitis Antiqua:* www.vitisantiqua1798.ch
Enjoy the noble Cornalin, a vine descendant from a vineyard dated to 1798.

Phrases

English	French	German
Hello, Hi!	Bonjour	hallo!
How are you?	Comment allez-vous?	Wie geht es?
Yes	oui	ja
No	non	nein
Thank you	merci	Danke schön.
Please	s'il vous plaît. (svp)	bitte
Good morning	bonjour	guten Morgen
Good afternoon	bon après-midi	guten Tag
Good evening	bonsoir	guten Abend
Please call a docor	Appelez un docteur svp	Rufen Sie bitte einen Doktor.
Hotel	hôtel	Hotel
Bread	pain	Brot
Coffee	café	Kaffee
Tea	thé	Tee
Vegetables	légumes	Gemüse
Beer	bière	Bier
Open	ouvert	offen
Closed	fermé	geschlossen
Street	rue, route	Strasse
Square	place	Platz
Pharmacy	pharmacie	Apotheke
Phone	téléphone	Telephon
Doctor	docteur	Arzt, Doktor
Flu	une grippe	Grippe

Public holidays

January 1	New Year's Day
March 19	St. Joseph's Day
	Easter
May /June	Ascension Day
May/June	Corpus Christi
August 1	National Holiday
August 15	Assumption
November 1	All Saints' Day
December 8	Immaculate Conception
December 25	Christmas Day

Index

Page 160: Dom, highest peak in the Valais.